CREATING A CHARACTER

CREATING A CHARACTER

A Physical Approach to Acting

Moni Yakim

with Muriel Broadman

BACK STAGE BOOKS
An imprint of Watson-Guptill Publications, New York

First published 1990 by Back Stage Books, an imprint of Watson-Guptill Publications, a division of BPI Communications, Inc., 1515 Broadway, New York, NY 10036.

Cover design by Bob Fillie.
Cover, title page photos by Elizabeth Marshall.
Book design by Publications Development Co. of Texas

Library of Congress Cataloging-in-Publication Data

Yakim, Moni.
    Creating a character : a physical approach to acting / Moni Yakim with Muriel Broadman.
        p.   cm.
    Includes bibliographical references (p.
    ISBN 0-8230-7552-4 :
    1. Acting.   I. Broadman, Muriel.   II. Title.
PN2061.Y   1990
792'.028—dc20   90-96
                                                                  CIP

Manufactured in the United States of America

Quality Printing and Binding by:
BERRYVILLE GRAPHICS
Box 272
Berryville, VA 22611 U.S.A.

First Printing, 1990

2 3 4 5 6 7 8 9 / 95 94 93 92 91

To Mina:
my colleague, my friend, my wife

Acknowledgments

To all of my students, who over the years have fueled me by their enthusiasm, openness, and willingness to explore, I give my love.

I thank the following artists who have encouraged me: Abraham Yakin, Samuel Avital, Etienne Decroux, Marcel Marceau, Stella Adler, John Houseman, Michael Kahn, Elizabeth Smith, Alan Schneider, Michael Langham, Harold Stone, Boaz Yakin, Erez Yakin, Theodore Mann, Colin O'Leary, Janet Bookspan, Elaine Housman, Peter Weller.

My gratitude to: Bonnie Jacobson, Walter Gidaly, Jonathan Lobl, Eli Housman.

Contents

PART III
CREATING A CHARACTER

Foreword

When I was in Paris in 1959, I met a young Israeli who had already achieved a considerable reputation as a director, an actor, and a mime. He was dedicated to the theater and remarkably charismatic. He wanted to come to the United States and I started by helping him with introductions and advice. The young man was Moni Yakim and his development has been astonishing.

Moni arrived in New York shortly afterward. He studied with me while he supported himself as a mime. He was fluent in Hebrew and French but his English was fairly new at that time. Mime aided him in his transition to the American stage.

After I watched Moni's work as a mime, I recommended that, excellent as he was, he abandon mime as a profession. It was clear to me that the limitations of mime as a theatrical form at that period would prevent him from achieving his potential as an actor. Mime, as I saw it, was an art of indication rather than of experience. As such, it could not let its practitioners project depths of true feeling. Without the ability to transmit genuine emotion to an audience, brilliant as his mime technique was, mesmerizing as he was as a mime, there would always be something missing which would make greatness elude him.

I have no doubt that Moni did not understand what I meant. He comprehended my words well enough, but he had a strong emotional commitment to mime and I was unable to reach him. However, he had utter faith in my judgment and devoted the next few years of his life to studying acting.

As a student, Moni appeared to absorb instantly theatrical concepts of great complexity. After he spent two years as a particularly apt pupil, I appointed him to teach "movement for actors," while he continued to study acting. I kept an eye on him. I could not help but be struck by his depth of understanding of stage physicality and characterization.

Characterization is a subject on which I have always placed enormous importance. Characterization can be taught from the outside in. The actor may use whatever will help his imagination create a character. Anything—a nose, a mask, a hat, a prop, a tone of voice, an environment, the art and architecture of his time. The actor's creative imagination creates a past that belongs to the character.

The actor doesn't exist; only the character exists. Characterization is the ability to understand what goes on in other people and identify with it. In certain circumstances the character reveals itself. If the house is burning and you take your hat and walk out, that's character. There is that big difference. You can't talk it away, you can't philosophize it away. You must be capable of doing it.

In the history of acting nobody has played himself. Now, there is a paradox here. There is a paradox in characterization. When the actor plays himself he is less interesting than when he plays a certain person.

Using basic concepts, Moni Yakim developed his "movement for actors" classes. I was able to observe how, step-by-step, through an innovative process he created himself, his unique physicalization of a character evolved. His techniques to attain characterization have been outstandingly successful in bringing out of his students emotional depth—disciplined emotion—to enrich whatever they do onstage. It is most rewarding to see this new direction in which he has travelled, inspiring and enabling students to become artists of the theater.

The new techniques which Moni has developed for actors, interestingly, have also taken him full circle in that they have allowed him to bring the richness of deep emotion to mime. Those mimes to whom he has taught his physicalization of a character have imbued their performances with a life that extends far beyond the mere "indications" so prevalent in most of their work only a generation ago.

Moni Yakim is an inspired teacher with an unusual grasp of how to develop a character for the stage. His ideas and practices, some of which this book details, make it required reading for every serious student of the theater.

Stella Adler

Introduction

You've just been given the part of Bluntschli in Shaw's *Arms and the Man*. At one point in the play your character enters in a state of such complete fatigue that he collapses onto a bed and falls asleep, even though it may cost him his life. You're enthusiastic and bursting with vitality—how do you portray such overwhelming exhaustion?

What about a more obvious physical acting challenge—the distorted body of Richard III or the Elephant Man? What about the powerful strength required to play Lenny in *Of Mice and Men* or the physical frailty of Laura in *The Glass Menagerie*? How can you transform yourself in order to create such characters, endowing them with the rich physical and emotional life that is at the heart of all good acting?

That was my problem. As a young actor, I knew what I wanted to do physically but I couldn't make my body do it. So I sought out and studied acting with some of the greatest master teachers in Europe and the United States. I learned body movement analysis, I learned intellectual concepts, and I learned emotional exercises. But I didn't learn what I needed to know.

I did, however, discover something about different acting approaches: most techniques deal with the emotional life of a character

1

but never deal with how the actor is expected to create a physical life. Many acting conservatories relegate this responsibility to teachers who conduct classes in something called "movement for actors," which often means a class in dance, aerobics, or acrobatics.

My approach to acting offers an understanding of character and entry to the emotional life of a character through the body. The process outlined in this book is designed to help the actor create a character of rich complexity and dimension for the stage.

But this book is not only for the actor—it serves the director, the teacher, and all students of theater. It details a unique approach to acting that concentrates on physical expression. The actor learns how to create a character physically and express emotions physically.

After all, the actor's ability to understand and portray a character lies at the heart of all acting technique. Acting *is* characterization.

An audience under the spell of a fine actor is satisfied it is in the presence of a human being who has subtleties, shadings, and a multiplicity of levels and dimensions. On the other hand, when an audience observes imitators or impersonators, regardless of the performers' skill, the audience is always aware these actors represent someone else. Their effort and talent are channelled into expressing behavior which is perceived to be not their own.

Imitation, no matter how skillful, can never be a true art form. Possessing no depth, imitation is limited in the dimensions necessary to art. Acting is *being* rather than exhibiting. As an actor you do not imitate the character. The qualities and behavior of the character must integrate themselves into your own being. By thinking, feeling, and behaving like the character, you achieve unity with it. You become the character.

Onstage you are never yourself: it is not *your* name which is listed in the script; the character's background is not yours. The character springs from the author's concepts and lives in a world created by the playwright. The playwright's idea of the character is projected through the character's dialogue and relationships.

It is through the characters' actions that the ideas in a play are communicated. For instance, a theme may be suggested by a play's central setting—the "Bus Stop," the "Glass Booth," or the "Cabaret"—but without characters' actions filling the stage, the play's ideas can not be expressed. The environment is chosen to evoke characters' actions.

All actors must study the meaning of the play and the function of their specific role. Why is the character in the play? How does the character serve the play's idea?

The job of an actor is to give the author's concept of the character flesh, blood, and inner life. This is accomplished through an understanding and development of the character's psychological, emotional, physical, environmental, and social conditions—past and present. All these elements combine to make the character complete.

Physicalization, my focus in this book, means to reveal a character to an audience through the use of the body. The deeper and more complete your physicalization of the character, the more human and believable the role becomes.

"Physicalizing a character" does not mean that you have to move constantly like an acrobat on a trampoline. Physical expression is as important in its stillness as in its movement, and no less expressive. Whether in movement or at rest, physical expression must grow out of the nature of the character you portray.

My physical approach to acting uses the body to create a concrete and tangible character. But it's not just the way the character's head is held or the spine curved or the arms extended. It's all this and more.

How do you, as an actor, look for a character?

Perhaps you read through your lines in the play, you get some ideas, and you believe you're ready to start trying to act the part. Then, as you work on the role, you find that its essence keeps slipping through your fingers. You begin to feel lost. You ask yourself, "What is it that eludes me? Why is my portrayal devoid of life?"

You grope for some clue that will put you truly in touch with the character on a deep, vibrant level. Perhaps this is when you finally discover that your analytical, intellectual comprehension of the role is not serving you. You sense you must somehow reach your character viscerally through the emotions, and yet everything you try seems forced and artificial.

Suddenly, when you least expect it, you "get it": an instinctive grasp of the character overwhelms you in a surge of emotion. Maybe you found the role's truth by suddenly discovering how the character brushes his teeth or the way she says "Gesundheit" and covers her mouth. You exclaim, "That's it! I've got it!" And you don't quite know how, but the truth is that you don't possess the character—it possesses you—and from that moment you are its prisoner. For an actor there is no better feeling.

Your character has taken over your thoughts and emotions. Automatically, a space has opened within yourself into which the life of the character flows.

Integrating with the character, mastering it in depth, means that what you do in a situation will always correspond truthfully to the needs and intentions of the play. You'll know how to behave within given circumstances, how to function within your environment, how to listen to your partner, and what action to take.

When you interpret a role, you look for the character's "truth." Here, I use the word "truth" to mean the endowment of the character with particular traits and behavioral patterns belonging specifically to that character. You make choices of interpretation by clear insight into the character's nature without imposing inconsistent traits on it. The more detailed and deep your treatment in the physicalization of the character, the richer and more colorful the character grows.

My physical approach to creating a character owes much to two of the greatest influences on my work. My technique tries to combine the best of both worlds—Etienne Decroux's insights into pure physical motion and Stella Adler's methods of unearthing organic emotional truth.

As a young actor I studied with Etienne Decroux. The "father of modern mime," he was recognized as the leading scientist in the field of body movement analysis. Working with him at his studio in Paris for five years as a student and a member of his company, I fell in love with mime and concentrated my efforts on gaining mastery of my body. Through these studies I also reached an insight into the philosophy and work methods of Antonin Artaud, Gordon Craig, Vsevolod Meyerhold, and Charles Chaplin—all instrumental in the development of Decroux's ideas on movement.

The turning point in my perception of physicalization occurred after Stella Adler saw me perform with Decroux's company. She strongly urged me to abandon mime, at least temporarily, because she believed mime did not reach the heart of characterization. She explained that in her observations mime tended to sketch or indicate a character rather than inhabit or live it. After studying with Ms. Adler, one of America's foremost interpreters of Stanislavsky, I began to understand what she meant.

I first explored my ideas in Ms. Adler's conservatory when she offered me the chance to teach movement to actors. I remembered my own experiences in such classes, and instead of leading my students in some simple dance steps, stretches, or stylized period gestures, I immediately had them exploring different ways to physicalize well-known dramatic characters, but without language. Ultimately, they worked on complete scenes, still without using words. I learned what worked well and what didn't. From these experiences I developed methods of teaching actors how to identify with a character, giving them techniques to utilize their bodies.

Through the years my explorations have deepened and broadened in scope. The value of my process has proven itself with my acting students at the Juilliard School, Yale University's School of Drama, Circle-in-the-Square's training program, Stella Adler's Theater Conservatory, and at my own Performance Theatre Center.

This book is a distillation of the more important conclusions I have reached over the years. I offer it to you in a form that, while comprehensive, is condensed to include only what is meaningful. Everything here—theory and exercises—has been tested and its effectiveness demonstrated.

The process described here is do-able and real. It helps overcome the usual difficulties in achieving physicalization. When you've explored these studies fully, you will be ready to portray any character in any play, from Anne Frank to Medea, from Willy Loman to Macbeth.

HOW TO USE THIS BOOK

Creating a Character is a basic guide to acting that will complement the techniques with which you may be working currently as well as any training you've acquired in the past. Although you, as an individual, will find much in this book you will profit from—concepts, approaches, and physical exercises—whenever possible, work with a group.

There are almost always other actors who will be glad to work with you to expand their techniques and hone their skills. Get together with them. Form a workshop. A group will provide feedback, criticism, an audience for whom to perform, and an increase in energy. If you are already in a class that works with the ideas and exercises in this book so much the better. By going over this material you will deepen your understanding of what is involved in physicalization.

The book is divided into three sections that form separate courses of study.

PART I: Looking In.   You begin the acting process by understanding yourself. In order to understand all the dimensions of a character, you must identify the character's traits with your own by *looking in*side yourself. Having established your common humanity with the character, you then turn to . . .

PART II: Looking Out.   You explore how the outside world—different elements of nature, animals, and objects—can be applied to make the transformations necessary to developing viable characters.

PART III: Acting.   This is a natural evolution of what you learn in Looking In and Looking Out. You act different roles from the canon of dramatic literature, integrating your self-knowledge and your physical comprehension of the world.

Some of the studies will require more than one session, possibly several sessions. The basic structure of the sessions is not always consistent. However, consistency has been maintained where it is helpful. Where consistency confers no particular benefit, the points to be made in a given study determine its form. The rules of the structure emerge from the study itself. The prime rule is to be open to all possibilities.

Parts I, II, and III have different purposes. Accordingly, the work sessions for each are structured differently. Furthermore, within each part the format varies according to the requirements of the subject. For example, the first study in Part I requires practice assignments which are not necessary for the other studies.

When you move from Part I to Part II you must clear your mind of everything that preceded the new study. It is as if you are taking off your clothes, folding them carefully, and putting them aside. You have a new outfit for Part II, and you will not go back for the first set of garments until you are ready for Part III where you will mix and match your items of apparel.

It has long been apparent to me as a teacher of acting that the ideal course of instruction offers a combination of theory and practice. It is necessary to understand the concepts on which the principles of acting are based—specifically, in this instance, creating a character through physicalization. Therefore, I have been careful to explain the ideas which underlie every aspect of what I have set forth.

Remember that while the theory is important, practice of the exercises is equally so. All the theory in the world amounts to just so many words on paper unless you take the opportunity to explore and experience bodily—concretely—what the theory establishes with the abstraction of words.

THE EXERCISES: SOME TIPS TO REMEMBER

Before you roll up your sleeves and get down to work, browse through the opening chapters to each section to get a feel for the underlying concepts that I discuss. Then go back and read those sections more thoroughly, but still only to absorb ideas, not to think about applying them as yet. After you are comfortable with the point of view and purpose of the study, you are ready to start work.

Studies are not selected at random. Each is designed to help you grow in a particular area. In some sections I have introduced a greater number of exercises than in others. These may seem like unnecessary duplications but they are not. They reinforce each other. The extra examples will not only be helpful in this regard but may serve as models for further study.

No matter how practical these acting exercises are for the actor, they are designed to spark some inspiration and creativity as well. If the imagination is not triggered by one example, it may be ignited by another. You don't know which exercise will turn you on until you actually experience each one.

As you begin to work on the exercises, remember that the voice and body are one integral unit. Accordingly, in most of your work you will use the voice as well as the body. Without being forced in any way, the voice should emerge naturally, and in any form: sighing, groaning, grunting, laughing, screaming, singing. . . . If it does not need to be released, there is no need to force it. On the other hand, if the voice demands release but is not freed, your body will remain suppressed. You'll notice that tension in the voice curtails the body's freedom of expression.

When actual words are used they should flow from the depth of the character or circumstances. Language should never be used to explain the situation but be an inseparable part of it. When you use words, don't grope to find the best vocabulary or intellectualize. Use only those words that spring almost unconsciously from an emotional impulse—unless, of course, you are performing a scene.

It is preferable to work in a room or studio bare of furnishings. If a chair or any other furniture or prop is to be used, it will be indicated in the given study. Otherwise, sit, lie, and move in open space. Don't rely on furnishings to express yourself. Your body and the surrounding space alone should be enough to meet the challenge of physicalization. Your imagination can expand to transform the open space into any environment.

Bear in mind that no matter how deeply you delve into your study, you never allow physical harm to yourself or others. I once witnessed an actor lose control and literally start beating his head against a wall. On another occasion, an actor choked his partner and physical injury was barely prevented. This kind of thing is an absolute no-no.

Follow the outlined procedures as closely as possible. Don't hesitate to refer to the concepts outlined in each section's introductory material when questions arise. Every now and then review the entire set of concepts.

Finally, you should realize that as an actor there is no way you can judge whether your exercise has been successful. What you learn from the work itself is the most genuine reward. Satisfaction will come from the experience of living and working within this process. Welcome the deep experience when it occurs, but don't despair if a new profound insight is not attained in every session. You cannot preconceive an end result. I do believe, however, that the benefits you will reap from these experiences will accumulate within you and become part of your being.

PART I

LOOKING IN

1

Approaching
the Selves

One of the functions of a performing artist is to illuminate the characters in a play—to give them an inner life so that their existence has meaning for an audience.

Feelings are universal. Everyone has them. By understanding your own feelings and identifying them, you can recognize the feelings of your assigned character. This identification process serves as the basis for my physical approach to creating a character. This is the process I've outlined in this section.

An actor must study the aspects of his or her nature by *Looking In,* by exploring the *self.* In this first part, I would like you to look at your total personality as if it were a jewel. Each facet refracts light differently to the beholder's eye. Each facet is necessary to the structure of the polished stone if the full potential of the gem is to be revealed.

For the purposes of this process, I would like you to focus on only six of the many aspects of yourself. Through my experiences I have found that these six *selves* embody the most important qualities every actor needs in order to be a well-rounded performer.

You must fragment your totality so as to isolate and study each of these *selves* separately. Each aspect of *self* must be worked on as an independent unit. As you study each *self,* work on it as if it were the only facet of your personality. Focusing on each aspect separately strengthens your emotional totality, just as working on specific muscles cannot help but improve overall body tone.

Which are the *selves* I have selected? They are:

- the *vulnerable self*
- the *instinctive self*
- the *social self*
- the *trusting self*
- the *unresolved self*
- the *decisive self*

No *self* is 100 percent "pure." The *vulnerable self,* for example, besides the obvious trait of vulnerability, also encompasses sensitivity. The *instinctive self* embodies spontaneity and believability. The *social self* emphasizes control. The *trusting self* contains openness, confidence, and abandon. The *unresolved self* includes dramatic tension. The *decisive self* has determination and the courage to take risks.

Can these qualities be learned? Yes! The techniques offered in this section can turn these concepts and abstractions into a practical and useful reality.

Although you may gain many psychological insights as you explore your *selves* through this process, this self-knowledge is intended to enrich your characterizations onstage. Remember that the goal of all these exercises must always be the complete, sensitive physicalization of a character.

THE LOOKING IN EXERCISES: SOME TIPS TO REMEMBER

Throughout all the *Looking In* exercises stay yourself. Don't "act." Go with your feelings of the moment. Do not be pressured into a preconceived mold. Stay free of all outside influences.

As you're probably aware, most actors are told quite early in their training that their bodies and voices are the instruments on which they play their part. Therefore, actors are exhorted to stay fit and are taught stretching and vocal warm-ups. I have devised some exercises for this section that are entirely different. They are not warm-ups as such. In addition to preparing the body, they help to establish the emotional climate for the work that follows.

Like a violin which must be tuned before it is played, both your physical instrument *and* your emotional resources must be prepared and attuned to the needs of each *self* workshop. Therefore, every session in the *selves* begins with what I call a *Tuning In* exercise. The *Tuning In* exercises have been individually chosen to promote an easier exploration of each *self.* Even though I have created varied exercises for each *self,* they are *always* preceded by a Tuning In exercise.

You will notice that these tuning exercises bear little resemblance to the *Tuning Up* exercises in Parts II and III. Nevertheless, whatever you do, don't skip these exercises or like a tone-deaf tenor in a choir, you'll be hopelessly out of tune.

2

The Vulnerable Self

There is an old Arabic saying that "man is as strong as iron, as hard as stone, and as fragile as a rose." It is this fragility that makes audiences empathize and involve themselves in the life an actor creates onstage. Some weakness—implicit or overt—is a quality audiences can understand and share. It is ironic that vulnerability, the one quality a person is most likely to conceal, is at the same time the one characteristic that most allows an audience to identify with an actor.

Audiences may admire Superman and cheer him on as some fulfillment of their fantasy but they know he does not need their support. Only when his invincibility comes into doubt—when he's faced with Kryptonite or he can't find a phone booth to make the change from Clark Kent—do audiences become emotionally supportive. Not until then do they feel at one with him as a fallible being; not until then is their involvement that of participants rather than spectators. Without vulnerability, audiences may applaud a performer's acting technique but all the actor's virtuosity will not make them care. Therefore, it is a professional requirement that all actors learn to use their vulnerability.

The *vulnerable self* workshop is the most important of the workshops in *Looking In*. Until you rediscover and become aware of your *vulnerable self* you will have difficulty fully experiencing all the other aspects of your acting education. As an actor, you must make this your first task. The more care and attention you give this study, the better base you will have for the studies that follow.

Experiencing your own vulnerability will let you identify and experience the vulnerability of a character. And just as importantly, inhibitions which restrict your performance will be overcome through the process. If you remain open to life, you remain vulnerable.

There are many areas of potential vulnerability. My technique concentrates on one aspect of vulnerability to which actors are particularly prone: the pressures generated by society's standards of physical beauty.

When society decrees that small noses and close-set ears are desirable, your Jimmy Durante schnozzola or Clark Gable ears can blight your world. In adolescence, if your sexual progress was at a rate different from that of your peers, most likely you were self-conscious and ashamed. Even as adults, if your physical dimensions do not compare favorably with those of Mr. or Miss America, if your complexion is less than flawless, if you are a bald man or a woman with facial hair, you may have felt you have somehow failed. Society's intolerances and prejudices make themselves excruciatingly clear.

Having a large nose in a society of small noses, or being black in a white society, or female in a male society, or any combination thereof, obviously does not make you less human or less able to contribute to the world in general and the theatre in particular. However, if you let your deviation from society's standards become a blemish, you become distorted. If you are fatter, thinner, scarred, or in any way different from the norm, and you let this steer your behavior—whether subtly avoiding mirrors or, much worse, failing to exploit your full potential—you are distorting your psyche to a greater extent than your so-called flaw has distorted your physical being.

Whether your perceived flaw is small or large, it can take on proportions that far exceed its real dimensions. It becomes magnified. Your obsession creates tensions which in turn cause tightness and rigidity as if you'd been stricken by some sort of physical paralysis.

Society has also set up psychological portraits of the ideal person and citizen whom you are encouraged to emulate. If you had been scolded as a child for being overly aggressive, overly withdrawn, overly emotional, overly trusting, then you may feel you are different, imperfect. Perhaps you retreated or covered up to prevent society from knowing your "weakness" and to protect yourself from feeling pain.

As an actor, you must look at yourself and into yourself. The work on the *vulnerable self* will help you uncover and dispose of layer after layer of concealing shrouds. You will bring to light what you had hoped never to see again.

Coming to terms with a situation you don't wish to confront can be a long, taxing process. Since childhood you may have been building defensive walls to isolate an embarrassment only you knew existed. Your shame could have its origins in what your young contemporaries considered laughable physical idiosyncracies. You were shorter or fatter or clumsier than they. Or you wore glasses or limped or stammered. So you pretended that these peculiarities were amusing or that you were indifferent to them or even that you liked having them—anything rather than admit that you wished you were different in some way.

Because the walls around private pain are so stout and so firmly established, many people take them as part of their very structure. They are in terror of seeing their defenses cracked, let alone demolished. The injuries caused by these perceived "flaws," or the magnification of them, have never been exposed to the air. They do not heal, however long they're protected.

It does not matter whether you mocked your own flaws, ignored them, or defended them. The diversion of energy required to conceal that lack of perfection prevents you from achieving your potential.

Without coming to terms with your flaws, real or imagined, the best in your talent is immobilized. Your ability to express yourself is blocked. You become static. You can move neither forward nor back. If, by an extreme effort, you manage to get off dead center and move in either direction, you cannot proceed far enough to satisfy yourself. The method each of us develops to deal with the pain of facing our flaws is part of what makes us unique individuals.

You therefore start with what and who you are. Now.

In the *vulnerable self* workshop you work with a flaw because this is a specific tangible problem—not some abstraction—that helps you to reach vulnerability in its wider scope. As you may be aware, many acting techniques attempt to break through a young actor's psychological defenses, even when this pseudo-psychiatry turns out to be harmful to the student. My process is different—

actors contact their vulnerability through their physical body, not through their psychic wounds and traumatic memories.

To reach vulnerability you must achieve nakedness. This is not the exhibitionism of nudity but the nakedness that will lay bare what you have hidden. As if they were garments, you learn to shed layers of inhibitions, prejudices, and even deep-seated mannerisms. These are not basic to your nature. You developed them to conceal your secret, distorted, tender injury. When you discover that this inner condition can survive public examination and, even more importantly, your own inspection, you will have achieved what this study intends for you as an actor. You will not be afraid to make a fool of yourself and you can develop a technique to express the vulnerability of a character.

More often than not, if this searching out of your flaw is carried to its inevitable conclusion, another most rewarding discovery is made. What you have always thought of as a defect in your physical or emotional make-up may not be a defect at all. What you are is not necessarily good or bad. It is simply what you are. Too many of us have let our lives be warped, even destroyed, because we have accepted society's values instead of working our way through them to a determination of our own standards.

Cyrano de Bergerac let society convince him that the length of his nose was so ludicrous no woman could see beyond it. Accordingly, he did not dare to woo Roxane for himself. He wasted his years on the fringes of her life, not realizing until it was too late that she could not have cared less about his obsession. Cyrano's problem was not his nose; it was how he felt about his nose.

If your nose by society's standards is too long, too short, too flat, too hooked, too pointed, too crooked—think about what you may do to minimize the attention that is paid to it. Do you arrange your hair to distract from it? When speaking to others, do you hold your head at an angle that makes your nose less conspicuous? Do you insist on flattering lighting when you have pictures taken? Perhaps you smile brightly or pontificate solemnly, so that you are remembered for your charm or wisdom, rather than for your nose?

You don't necessarily think about all this, but your attitudes and mannerisms color virtually everything you do. It is likely they have been created to conceal how vulnerable you are to the world's opinion and how deeply this opinion has wounded you. To deal with this you create a personality far removed from your true essence.

It hurts to chip away the stone that has hidden your most private, most tender being from yourself. The closer you come to your naked essence, the more you hurt. You want to draw back, to plaster up whatever cracks you have made, to pretend there is nothing behind the wall that is soft and crippled and grieving. This is what must be liberated and made whole so that you can be freed from the need to guard it, releasing your total energy for productive use.

Your best strengths as an actor will arise out of such personal exploration. What were once handicaps can become assets. Fear will be transformed into a flow of creativity.

A keen awareness of your *vulnerable self* clears the path to an understanding and acceptance of who you are, in all your facets. This acceptance of yourself will help you to identify and feel as the character and to understand why the character has a particular way of talking, eating, and so forth. It will enrich and sharpen your insight into the human condition.

THE VULNERABLE SELF EXERCISES

While you explore the *vulnerable self,* keep in mind that you are looking into yourself. You are immersed in a world that is all your own. The work is a personal experience.

Because there is so much ground to cover, this particular exploration must be allowed more time than is allotted to other *Looking In* studies. It may not be possible to adhere to a predetermined schedule: your progress and your internal rhythms must develop their own space in time, superseding a rigid timetable.

In the *vulnerable self* study it is crucial to maintain continuity. This study is designed to put you in touch with your vulnerability, which invariably awakens your consciousness to unresolved sensitivities and emotions. Interference with the orderly progress of the exercises can prevent you from achieving the maximum results: complete freedom from your inhibitions as an actor and identification with vulnerability in a character.

If you don't feel a particular *vulnerable self* work session has penetrated to the heart of a perceived personal flaw, or if the breakthrough has not been sufficiently effective in releasing you from its control, you may choose to continue working on it, or come back to this flaw after you have explored others. Even though at the end of this chapter I have provided eight model work sessions, you should not be surprised if you feel you want to do more. Repeat or create as many of these exercises as you feel necessary.

If you're working alone, use this book as your teacher, as if I'm speaking to you directly. If you're in a group, allow the instructor or leader to guide you through these exercises.

The *vulnerable self* sessions consist of three steps:

- Tuning In: Using the forces of nature as a step toward vulnerability.
- Focus: Magnifying and physicalizing a personal flaw.
- Practice: Working on the flaw in day-to-day life.

Tuning In

As with every exercise in Part I, Tuning In is the first step toward the *vulnerable self*. It leads you toward your own vulnerabilities and "tunes" you—sensitizes you to the feelings your flaw evokes in you.

I use the imagination instead of sense memory, as others might. In addition, I work through the metaphor of a force of nature: rain, fog, earthquake, and so on. Because nature's forces are impersonal, you do not feel under personal attack as you try to reach the walled-in emotions your flaw has developed.

This force of nature links you emotionally to the heart of the problem with unexpected speed. For example, the experience of being in an earthquake releases a tide of feelings which allow you to experience your physical vulnerability. Though the earthquake is created from your imagination, the experience is real. After you have felt this emotion and realized the earth has not swallowed you, you are ready to deal with your emotions in a more personal way.

When you work on minor flaws, choose comparably mild aspects of nature. Let's say you have a tiny mole on your face that does not evoke intense emotions. Therefore, you would select a force of nature that evokes an equivalent degree of intensity. For example, mist or a light rain would be a relatively mild natural force.

In subsequent sessions we go more deeply into flaws about which you'll have stronger feelings. As the intensity increases, you should select a more powerful aspect of nature. Finally, when we deal with elements of great magnitude—flood, tornado, earthquake, avalanche, fire—you will lose the ability to control your actions. However, remember it is not the force of nature that is the subject of this work but its effect on you, the person on whom this force is exerted. Not only is the natural force the work of the imagination but it must be physically enacted.

The way each Tuning In exercise works will be clear in the model sessions that follow. After you choose a force of nature, you will use your imagination to create fictive situations in which you are totally exposed to that force.

Whatever threatening situation you create, it is important that it be as remote as possible from your daily environment. You must then imagine this situation so intensely that the circumstances become vividly alive for you, not as a fiction but as a reality that becomes your whole world. You must live in the situation, physicalizing every aspect.

One example of a force of nature might be a storm at sea. You might imagine yourself in a lifeboat with a few other imaginary passengers. You might look back to the ship you've left and watch it sinking beneath the violent surface of the water. Is there anyone dear to you on board? What do you do? How do you react? Become aware of your own peril. You are tossed about like a toy. Try to keep from falling overboard. You might have to start bailing desperately. You grow exhausted. Are there any life preservers? How do you prevent the boat from capsizing? Where are the oars? Is there a radio to call mayday? It's becoming darker and colder. Do you huddle against each other? Wrap yourself in blankets? It's dark. The battering of the waves is unremitting. How does this effect you?

Allow yourself total freedom of expression in these Tuning In scenarios. Use words and vocal sounds such as screams, physical action—whatever develops naturally, without being forced.

Throughout the entire exploration of the situation, keep your senses alert. Your entire body tingles to the touch of nature's elements against your skin. With each different element of nature your imagination triggers your senses so you feel the rain, you hear the thunder, you smell the volcano's ash, you taste the snowflakes in your mouth.

Use the forces of nature that I've supplied as examples. If you're working with a group of fellow actors, take turns leading the others through the visualization of the situation, or follow the instructor's direction. If you're working on your own, feel free to create other circumstances as well which may have more immediacy for you and give you a new insight into your particular flaw. For instance, if it would inspire you better to be alone on a raft during the storm, go ahead and imagine that situation. In other words, don't feel bound by my sample situations—every participant can improvise circumstances if desired that are more personally alive. However, you should deal with the specific elements of nature that I've provided.

Focus: Magnifying and Physicalizing Your Personal Flaws

After you have explored an element of nature you will discover that you survived the forces that threatened you. You have the valid expectation you can survive the same intensity of forces which surge within you. You are more prepared to deal directly with your personal problem: you are ready to "focus" on your personal vulnerability. This is the essence of the *vulnerable self* study.

There are two phases to this procedure: the first is an internal process that requires you to sit quietly, calling forth some small physical defect at first, studying and magnifying it in your mind's eye. Then comes the second phase wherein you physicalize your exploration, bringing your flaw to life, exaggerating it, seeing how it modifies your behavior and distorts your being.

I'll repeat myself here because it is important: in your first sessions do not attempt to penetrate to the heart of a major flaw. You are too unprepared, too unprotected, too resistant to the scrutiny of your most private being, even from your own eyes. Start with what you consider a trivial defect—a crooked thumb, a scar on the arm, a small birthmark on the neck—flaws you have long since adjusted to and shrugged away.

If you're working with a group of actors, concentrate on your own work throughout each session. Do not be distracted by your fellow actors.

Sometimes the work differs from session to session. Any particular deviations in the procedures will be described.

Practice

As the familiar joke goes, practice is the way a musician gets to Carnegie Hall. For actors to be accomplished artists as well, they must do the same. At the conclusion of each session further assignments are given. These are of several types, depending on the subject. Most often, the assignment involves carrying the lessons learned in each session out into the real world for further exploration. Practicing the assignment between sessions is invaluable.

If you're working within a group, it is just as important to share your experiences with others and obtain their feedback. That's why every session after the first should begin with all workshop members sharing their experiences with each exercise. If you're working on your own, keep a diary of your reactions, observations, and feelings when practicing the assignment. Review your notes before proceeding with the next exercise.

THE VULNERABLE SELF: FIRST MODEL SESSION

Tuning In—Mist

Always start standing up on your feet. Pick a spot in the room where you feel comfortable. If you want to walk around, that's all right, too. What is important is that you give your imagination over to your group's leader who will lead you into action by describing the following situation. If you're alone, read the situation through and then proceed into action. In either case, you should fully act out the scenario in as detailed a manner as possible.

> You are getting into a car, starting it up, and beginning to drive. Is it a compact car, a truck, or a van? Is it old or the latest model? Is it a pleasure to drive or a pain in the butt? Watch the road and scenery go by until soon the city is far behind you.
>
> You find yourself on a lonely road. You've never been here before. There are no road signs. Is the road paved? Is the area flat? Hilly? Wooded? Barren? What's it like on either side of the road? Sandy? Marshy? Rocky?
>
> Imagine it's twilight and slowly a mist comes rolling in from nowhere. It envelopes the road, then the car. Your car stalls. You try to start it again. And again and again. It's no use. So you look around but there's no one around. You decide to abandon the car and go for help. You get out of the car and into the mist. You start walking through the mist, trying to follow the road. Then the mist thickens into fog . . .

Focus on Personal Vulnerability

While you hold on to the feelings you've gotten from the Tuning In situation, concentrate on some minor physical problem or trivial defect that disturbs you now or that disturbed you in the past: a wart, freckles on your shoulders, the way your hair stands up or falls. Choose only one flaw to focus on. The flaw you select is personal to you. No one else need know what it is.

Phase 1—Magnifying the Flaw.   Look at the flaw you selected. Think about it: where it came from, how long you've had it. If it is where you can't see it, visualize it with your mind's eye. Consider it more and more as part of your person, allowing the feelings that came to you earlier to merge with your feelings about the flaw. Don't control or direct them. It is your emotions that will lead you into the vulnerable condition.

Stay in this state for some twenty minutes. Whether the flaw is visible or in the mind's eye, the longer you stare at it the more it takes on exaggerated dimensions, as if you see it through a magnifying glass. The longer you stay with it, the more you connect it with your original feelings about it. The flaw is here, with you. As you magnify it, you no longer deny that it is part of you.

Phase 2—Physicalizing the Flaw.   It's important that you not lose any of the emotional intensity that has been built up in this linkage with your flaw. Try to carry it with you as you go through specific actions—sitting, walking, putting on an imaginary shirt or dress, combing your hair—and as you do so, try to find natural ways of exposing your flaw. Let's say, for example, you have a crooked finger. Instead of hiding your hand as you usually do, shake hands with all your fingers unconcealed. Show your finger when you hold a cup, pick up a pencil, tie a shoe. Sit with your hand on the table instead of in your lap.

It is in this part of the workshop that you allow your emotions to go all the way. If you feel that one action—say, exposing your flaw through the holding of a cup—wants to be prolonged as if frozen in space for three, four, five minutes, then sustain the movement. What governs the time is the necessity for the emotions to reach a peak of intensity. This phase gives you the space to make a breakthrough into the raw feelings that until now were inhibited by the flaw. If you need thirty, forty-five, or even sixty minutes to achieve this result, take it . . .

Throughout my years teaching this process I have found that it is virtually impossible to predict how students will react in these sessions. A most circumspect young woman, the last person in the world from whom I should have expected an emotional outburst, exploded into tears. Even while she was crying, she said she felt a release from tension she had rarely felt. On the other hand, a usually excitable young man with a low boiling point merely tightened his jaw and looked grim. Another told me he didn't know whether he would come back to my class, but he did, and over the next weeks developed an assurance I hadn't seen before. Everyone's reaction is different.

Practice

Now that you've made a contact with your vulnerability through exposing a personal physical flaw, carry your experience into everyday life. For an entire week live your problem. Expose your flaw in every situation you find yourself in, whether it's in the street, in a restaurant, at home, at school, or at work. Discover ways to avoid your habit of hiding it.

Since the problem you selected is a minor one, your experience during this week vis-a-vis other people may range from the irritating to the comic. Don't reveal your experiences to anyone or discuss them with fellow actors from your group until the next meeting. If you're working alone, make notes of your experiences. If you want to discuss them, it will have to be with someone who has gone through something similar because it's no use talking to an actor who hasn't been through it.

THE VULNERABLE SELF: SECOND MODEL SESSION

Sharing the Experience

It is important to talk about your *Looking In* assignment, to share what you went through. You'll realize that we all have hidden problems of which we are greatly ashamed, and by which our personalities have been distorted. This gives you more confidence in yourself. When you share common pains and common secrets, you'll find you are not alone. This is comforting and reassuring.

Talk about what you went through since the last session as you walked through your world "living your flaw." Tell what you did, how other people reacted, how you felt. Were you tempted to stop and hide your flaw as usual? Did you stop? If you continued, what drove you?

Once you've shared your experiences, move on to the new Tuning In exercise.

Tuning In—Cold Wind

Find a spot in the room in which you can work. The force of nature you will explore in this session is a cold wind. As with the last situation, have a designated group member lead the visualization, or if you're on your own, read through once or twice before using your own imagination to supply the details.

> You are in the middle of the wilderness on a camping trip. You are fishing in a river far from your campsite. Are you in a canoe? On the river bank? Wading in the shallows? You choose.
>
> It's a beautiful day. The sun is pleasant on your bare back. Absorbed in your pleasure, you only gradually become aware that the sky has turned overcast and a cold wind has started to blow. You realize you are cold, and you remember that all your warm clothing is back at camp.
>
> The wind picks up, colder and stronger. You wonder if you should try to get back to camp before the oncoming storm? You look around at the riverbanks to see if there's any place to find shelter. The wind chills you, buffets you, knifes through your clothing stinging your skin. Your ears burn, your eyes water. Where can you go? What do you do? How does it feel?

Once again, hold on to what you are feeling.

Focus on Your Personal Vulnerability

For this second session, select a flaw that bears more importantly on the making of your personality than the one you chose last time. Do not choose a major flaw yet. Focus on it as you did in the first session.

Phase 1—Magnifying the Flaw.   Look at your flaw. Think about it. Enlarge it until you no longer can deny it is part of you.

Phase 2—Physicalizing the Flaw.   Keeping the emotional intensity as you did in the first session, expose your flaw, find ways you can show it off, use it, make it obvious. Physicalize it in every way you can and let your emotions go all the way.

Practice

As you did last time, live your flaw in your day-to-day life and write down your experiences and be ready to discuss them when your group next meets.

THE VULNERABLE SELF: THIRD MODEL SESSION

Sharing the Experience

Once again, talk about your experiences trying to expose this last flaw. Discuss how you walked through your world "living your flaw." Detail what kinds of actions you took that were different from your normal modes of behavior. Relate how other people reacted, and how their reaction made you feel.

Once you've shared your experiences, move on to the new Tuning In exercise.

Tuning In—Flood

Find your space in the room and explore fully the following situation:

> You are sleeping in a house that you have recently bought when you are awakened by the sounds of thunder and the steady drumming of a rainstorm, which soon turns into a torrential downpour. You look out a window at the happy little brook that, before you had gone to sleep, had gurgled lightly by, about twenty feet away from your door.
>
> That tiny creek is now a raging river, tossing boulders about like matchsticks, carrying full-grown trees in its swollen power, slamming them against the little footbridge splintering it into pieces that are now completely submerged. The water rises higher, foot by foot, sloshing closer and closer to the house.

You go to the basement steps and see the cellar is filling up, relentlessly. How do you keep the water from rising to the ground floor?

Now the water is coming in under the door. Rising up from the basement. What prized personal possessions should you try to salvage? Your guitar? Your baby pictures? Your first editions?

The water is still rising. Retreat up the stairs to the next floor. Witness the devastation to your house and its contents. Everything you own in the world is being submerged. Can the house survive? Can you?

Hold onto your emotional state as you proceed.

Focus on Personal Vulnerability

Now you are ready to tackle what you consider your most serious physical flaw.

Phase 1—Magnifying the Flaw. As in the two previous sessions, think about your flaw. Enlarge it until you no longer can deny it is part of you.

Phase 2—Physicalizing the Flaw. Keeping the emotional intensity as you did previously, expose your flaw, finding and exploring ways you can show it off, use it, make it obvious. Physicalize it in every possible manner and let your emotions go all the way.

Practice

By focusing on a major physical "flaw" you have brought your problem into your consciousness. This awareness must have an effect on you. However, during the coming week, relax your concerns about this problem and try not to think about it.

Instead, your objective this week is to shake yourself up by breaking the mold in which your life has been set. You want to get rid of ideas and influences which have constricted you —whether they are good or bad.

This week is your golden opportunity to break all your personal rules and to do it without any trace of guilt. This is your chance to eat three triple-scoop banana splits in one sitting if you feel like it. Add as much hot fudge, chopped nuts, whipped cream, and maraschino cherries as you desire. Or stuff yourself with all the potato chips, salted peanuts, or pretzels you can eat. Enjoy all the pizza or lemon meringue pie you've ever wanted. And relish every mouthful.

In this one wonderful week you can read the books and see the films you've always avoided out of fear of their effect on your psyche. Go out of your way to indulge yourself in forbidden fruits of the body and soul.

Open yourself to problems you've been avoiding—with family members, co-workers, friends, enemies.

Disrupt every area of your life that has become routine. Dress the way you've always wanted to. Forget your compulsive promptness. Deliberately destroy as many behavioral patterns as you see in yourself. Use your left hand instead of your right. Dawdle where you would ordinarily run. Run where you would saunter.

In only two areas are there taboos. Shun whatever will dull your consciousness or your ability for self-observation—alcohol or drugs, for instance. For this experience to serve its purpose, your mind must be completely clear.

You must not harm yourself or anyone else or destroy property whose destruction you'll regret later on. No matter how much you want to punch your boss in the teeth or toss the baby out the window or kick the dog or throw a brick through the TV screen . . . don't! During this week, try not to get arrested.

Indulge yourself until you are sated physically and emotionally—and all without guilt.

As in the previous exercises, write down your experiences so you may be prepared to share them before tackling the next force of nature.

THE VULNERABLE SELF:
FOURTH MODEL SESSION

Sharing the Experience

Before continuing with the fourth session, once again discuss the experiences you had trying to alter your behavior. How hard was it? How far did you go? Was it fun? In what ways did the week surprise you? Did you find certain experiences that you had looked forward to disappointing? Did other experiences that you always dreaded turn out less frightening than you had expected?

This self-knowledge is crucial. It is the bridge to knowing the others whom you wish to portray.

Tuning In—Earthquake

After your discussion get on your feet and find a place in the room in which you can work. Get ready to explore the following situation:

> You are visiting an archaeological site. Are you in a desert? A jungle? A grassy plain? Walk around the site and try to memorize every physical detail of the structure. Is it a house or a whole village? A crumbling palace or a once glittering temple? How big is it? How decayed?
>
> Walk amid the ruins trying to soak in the past. Then suddenly you sense a trembling around you. You don't know why you feel dizzy. The earth begins vibrating harder and you can't seem to find your balance. The tremor inexorably reaches its climax. The ground and everything around you is shaking violently.
>
> All at once, right before you, the earth cracks open in a wrenching, ear-splitting groan.

Hold on to what you are feeling and move on.

Focus on Personal Vulnerability

Once again work on the same major personal physical flaw that you used last time.

Phase 1—Magnifying the Flaw.   Focus on your flaw and tell yourself over and over, "I hate it! I don't want it! I can't stand it!" Build up a negative emotional reaction to the flaw. Imagine what might be the most extreme act you would commit in order to destroy it or correct it.

Phase 2—Physicalizing the Flaw.   Imagine a situation in which your flaw has made you most vulnerable. For example, you are rejected by an employer or a prospective lover because of your flaw. Enact this situation without words imagining the other participants. If you're in a group, work by yourself and don't pay attention to what other actors may be doing at the same time. When you're firmly in the situation that would make you most vulnerable to your physical flaw, conceive of a second situation in which you correct your flaw or even rid yourself of it completely in the same way you did earlier in the exercise.

Practice

For the next session, prepare a piece based on what you did in Phase 2. This should be four or five minutes long and have a beginning, a middle, and an end. Your piece should demonstrate what you'd like to do with this particular flaw. Feel free to use vocal sounds or words—whatever is natural in dealing with the flaw. Props and other actors are imaginary.

THE VULNERABLE SELF: FIFTH MODEL SESSION

Sharing the Experience

Present to the group the piece you prepared. Don't be daunted if your work looks comical to others, even though your intent is serious. Or you may choose to be funny. Comedy can be as cathartic as tragedy. What's important is that you see how other actors have dealt with their vulnerabilities. Then prepare yourself for the next step.

Tuning In—Quicksand

Find an area of the room and physicalize the following situation:

> You are walking across a wide, open meadow to a distant destination. The terrain is barren of trees and shrubs, supporting only sparse grasses. As you proceed, the earth turns to mud under your feet. You sink in it up to your ankles. You struggle on, hoping to find firmer footing. You find yourself being pulled downward. You realize you are in quicksand, with nothing to cling to and no knowledge of what to do.

Focus on Personal Vulnerability

Phase 1—Magnifying the Flaw.   Choose the same major physical flaw that you've worked on in the last two sessions. Look at it if it's physically possible, focusing on it, as you did with the minor flaw in the first session. If it's not visible to you, visualize your flaw in your mind's eye. In either case focus on it for approximately twenty minutes, enlarging it, magnifying it, until you can accept it as a part of you.

Phase 2—Physicalizing the Flaw.   Then, without losing any of your emotional intensity, do as you did in the first session, moving about the room trying to exhibit your flaw in a variety of activities—cooking, playing a game, getting dressed. The point here is to find the raw emotions that this flaw has engendered. If one action causes a particularly powerful response, continue it for as many minutes as necessary. This exploration could continue for a half-hour, or even an hour.

Practice

In the coming week, do everything possible to expose the flaw in your day-to-day life. At work, with your family, at a restaurant or in your living room. Try to make it as noticeable as possible. Keep a journal or diary of your observations to share with the group before the next session, or to review on your own if you're working solo.

THE VULNERABLE SELF: SIXTH MODEL SESSION

Sharing the Experience

Start this session as in the second—by discussing your experiences during the week with your fellow actors if you're in a group. The idea is to realize how we all have vulnerabilities—even without a workshop of fellow actors you should be starting to feel less self-conscious and more free with yourself.

Tuning In

Find a comfortable spot in the room. Begin to imagine yourself in the following situation and then go into action:

> It's winter. And you have just acquired a house in the mountains. You have walked into the nearest village, several miles away, for supplies. You are on the way back, on the only road. The temperature plummets. The road, which was barely passable before, is now an unbroken sheet of ice. The ice is slippery and affords no traction for your feet. It seems as if you're not getting anywhere.
>
> Suddenly you see your house, still a couple of miles away in the distance, and you notice smoke rising from it. You try to walk faster but the road is solid ice. Perhaps someone dear to you is in the house?

Are they safe? You watch as fire starts to spread throughout your house. You must reach the house to help rescue your loved ones and to salvage your favorite possessions. But you must go by the only path— the ice-covered road.

Hold onto the emotions you're experiencing and move on to the next phase.

Focus on Personal Vulnerability

Phase 1—Magnifying the Flaw.   Select the same flaw you chose in the last three sessions and focus on it in the same way. Enlarge it, think about it, watch it.

Phase 2—Physicalizing the Flaw.   Now, moving around the room, try to hide the flaw in an exaggerated manner. If this draws attention to it, the resulting situation could be comical. That is alright. You do not have to avoid being funny.

Practice

Create a four-to-five minute piece, as you did in the fourth session. It should be based on your attempts to hide your flaw in an exaggerated way. Before you begin the Tuning In exercise for the next session, act out your piece for your fellow group members, or just for yourself.

THE VULNERABLE SELF: SEVENTH MODEL SESSION

Sharing the Experience

Before you begin this session, present your short piece. Again this reinforces the idea that you are not alone with your vulnerabilities. Furthermore, your ability to put your own physical flaw to creative use will grow.

Tuning In—Heavy Hail

Get on your feet and find an area in the room to work. Imagine and physicalize the following situation in as much detail as you can:

You are taking part in a marathon race. (You may run in place or around the room.) You sense the other runners and the crowds lining the streets, cheering. You feel strong and little by little you're pulling away and running in front of everyone. Notice the neighborhood you're running through and the weather.

It starts to rain and the crowds are starting to thin out. As the rain turns to sleet, they disappear. . . . You keep running with the icy rain beating you. You are way ahead of the other runners, the crowd is gone, you are on streets you have never been on before. The sleet has become hail which is pelting you, battering you, bruising you.

You find yourself in a large, open stretch of road with no shelter anywhere in sight. You must go on, defenseless against the hail.

Hold onto the feelings you're experiencing and begin focusing.

Focus on Personal Vulnerability

Phase 1—Magnifying the Flaw.   This time you should focus on *all* your physical flaws. Think of every possible defect or distortion in your body, from your major problems down to the most trivial. It could be something as slight as the tilt of your head to one side, or the way one shoulder is a tiny bit lower than the other, or a slightly turned in foot. Brood on each one, enlarging it, exploring all its dimensions. Then move on to the next.

Phase 2—Physicalizing the Flaw.   Now move around the room as you did in previous sessions, exaggerating all these physical details. Mime as many activities as you can imagine—bowling, ice skating, reading a newspaper, cooking pancakes—in order to bring out all your physical tics.

Practice

For an entire week, experience intensely more of what you are by exaggerating everything. Even the color and pitch of your voice should become extreme. If your head tends to tilt, pull it to one side dramatically. If one shoulder is lower than the other, stress the lack of symmetry. Emphasize the turning in of the feet until both legs are distorted. Eat, sleep, work, go on a date and dance, but keep all these movements at their most exaggerated extreme.

As always, keep a record or an account of your feelings and experiences, your observations and anecdotes.

THE VULNERABLE SELF:
EIGHTH MODEL SESSION

Sharing the Experience

Take turns contributing your personal experiences during the past week in which you brought all your physical flaws out into the open. If you're working outside a group, share your observations with fellow actors who understand the process.

Tuning In—Tornado

Once more, stand and move to a clear space in the room in which to work. Fully imagine and enact the following situation:

> You are alone in the middle of a vast, open field on a plain—flat from horizon to horizon. Perhaps there's an outcropping of rocks or some brush. Notice how scrubby or clear the land is. What's the soil like? Dusty or wet?
>
> The sky darkens and you look off in the distance and notice a black smudge in the sky, right over the rim of the horizon. It is drawing nearer and now you know it is a tornado.
>
> The twister is snaking in your direction. The wind starts to howl. Dirt flies everywhere. The roaring intensifies. You look for a place to hide, but there is nowhere to go. Maybe you run or you lie down, hoping the tornado will pass you by. You hear it roaring closer, closer. The sound is deafening.

Hold onto your feelings and emotions and move on.

Focus on Personal Vulnerability

This session deals with emotional problems not originating from one's own physical condition. Think of what most embarrasses you. Are you ashamed of your speech patterns? Of your ethnic background? Of coming from the wrong side of the tracks? Does it still rankle deep inside that someone once called you stingy or stupid or thought you were completely devoid of a sense of humor?

Phase 1—Magnifying the Flaw.   Dredge up an incident in which you were deeply embarrassed or ashamed, or concentrate on a condition that makes you uncomfortable to think about. Focus on the feelings and emotions that arise until they fill you completely.

Phase 2—Physicalizing the Flaw.   React physically to the acute shame that overwhelms you. Pull in, tighten up, become one with your emotion. Act it out as much as possible, perhaps trying the same actions you'd attempted with your physical flaws.

Practice

Keep this major emotional problem in focus for an entire week. When you communicate with others, make sure that whatever you say stems from this problem, with the intention of accentuating rather than hiding it. For example, if you are self-conscious about being considered stingy, bargain effusively over the price of a dozen oranges. If you are self-conscious about being too buddy-buddy, start effusive conversations with everyone on the supermarket check-out line, in the bus, at the lunch counter. If you have been accused, with some truth, of vanity, steer all conversations to your triumphs, problems, work, hobbies, appearance.

Though this is the last model session in the vulnerable set, you can develop as many more studies as you feel necessary. Add workshops on different forces of nature, or repeat ones that you'd like to work on some more.

LOOKING BACK

The *vulnerable self* study hasn't been easy. It took courage to face up to the concealed flaws you've harbored for so many years. These distortions to your psyche, and the tightness, rigidity, and the diversion of your energies which they caused, kept you from identifying your main attribute as an actor. You have come out of the closet, learned to drop your inhibitions, and have lost the need for the mannerisms which were your armor and your stumbling blocks to creating the physical life of other characters. You are ready to explore other facets of yourself.

3

The Instinctive Self

In order to make you a social creature, your environment has conditioned you to smother your *instinctive self*. Ever since childhood, it's been, "Don't hit your little brother!" Or, "Let your guest have the last cookie!" and "Don't talk with your mouth full!" By the time you are an adult, you've forgotten your *instinctive self*.

Some of us never find it again. We don't know how to evoke the spontaneity, truth, and passion that are latent in our *instinctive self*. To draw on these elements for your craft, you must bring the *instinctive self* to the surface.

The *instinctive self* is that part of you which is the alert, unconscious energy that reacts to a stimulus, without the mind's interference. It is your primitive reaction, your uncalculated response to contact with the external world or to your inner urges. Your instincts are restricted by being able to do no more than react to whatever stimulates the senses and to the demands of such inner needs as hunger, sleep, copulation, and self-protection.

In order to reach your instincts, you must bypass intellect. Now that you have experienced the *vulnerable self*, you are ready to penetrate beneath your brain's perpetual command. Learning to know and trust your *instinctive self* will, at least at first, be blocked by your brain. All your life your intelligence has been observing everything that comes within its ken, acting upon its observations or storing the information. Your brain is entrenched in its power and will yield to instinct only with reluctance.

Dominance by the brain leads to over-intellectualization and analytical understanding, rather than instinctive response. Through the intellect you understand the character. Through the instinct you identify and become one with it.

To find your *instinctive self*, live in a realm where there are no laws, no standards of right or wrong. Look within yourself for a level of infancy, of innocence. There you have no concern for how you appear to others. Revert to a primitive state where you have no social image to adhere to.

The *instinctive self* exists dormant until a stimulus awakens it. It is indifferent to reason, recognizes no pattern of thought or behavior. Subtleties, sophistication, strategies are not part of your *instinctive self*. Like the infant, when you are ruled by the *instinctive self* your attention span and focus are minimal.

The *instinctive self* never plans. It is neither curious nor adventurous. It lives in a state of pure existentialism and spontaneity. It knows no past or future. All it knows is now. Its action is a reaction to the stimulus.

The reactions of your *instinctive self* cannot be conditioned, nor can learned patterns develop, for everything is for the first time, regardless of how often you have experienced it. The instinct is always correct at the time it expresses itself. Even if afterwards the consequences of reaction based on instinct should prove unfortunate, for now, for the moment itself, the reaction is justified. Your primitive reactions and the basic emotions they engender are the keys to spontaneity, truth, and passion.

As an actor, you want to merge your physical and emotional reactions—you want to avoid the analytic process of distinguishing between the instinctive and the emotional. To act instinctively is to act spontaneously. To act spontaneously is to act truthfully. The mind has planned no deceptive strategies. You reveal your state of being at the moment.

The three components—instinct, spontaneity, and truthfulness—are combined; they cannot be separated. The practice of the *instinctive self*, the releasing of your instincts, is what enables you as an actor to physicalize your character with increased truth, believability, and strength. The intensity of your reactions is the measure of the passion portrayed.

Real as your instincts are, they are intangible. How then do you grasp them? How do you make them concrete so that, as an actor, you can deal with them physically? By using your five senses as channels through which a stimulus can reach your inner being. Sights, sounds, tastes, and smells immediately impinge on your instincts. Your inner being is even aware.of the physical touches from the pressure of the atmosphere or the crisp air of morning.

Your sensory organs are located in various parts of your body, but the messages they transmit to the brain for analysis have their emotional impact in one place—the gut, or to be elegant, the solar plexus.

In concepts as ancient as those of the Yogic philosophies of India, or as contemporary as those of many modern dancers, the seat of the emotions is placed in the gut. Evidence of this abounds. "Gut reaction" is commonplace as an expression which recognizes this. Prolonged stress can result in peptic ulcers. Stage fright creates "butterflies in the stomach."

Not only is the gut the source of problems caused by instinctive reactions, it is also the center of energy, the trigger to initiate the reaction. It is the source from which your nerves send a flow of power to be translated into a specific reaction.

THE INSTINCTIVE SELF EXERCISES

There are many ways to trigger the *instinctive self.* Acting methods usually go two routes: direct physical stimulation of the body through the senses or psychological stimulation through the mind, the memory, and the emotions. Direct stimulation of the senses doesn't require much explanation—you arouse the senses through touch, smells, sounds, and visual images—while examples of the latter might be hearing that a dear relative has just died, or imagining that you have just won $18,000,000 in the lottery, or that your neighbor has just totalled the brand new car you bought yesterday. Your initial reactions, before you cost the consequences, is identical with the reaction to a physical stimulus. However, since we are dealing in this book with physical aspects of acting rather than psychological reactions, we'll stay away from the second type and the invention of circumstances.

Unlike the *vulnerable self* where you can create imaginary environments—rain, sun, a pond, a field, a restaurant—in this study you create no inner impulses, not even hunger or desire for sleep. Here you deal only with what rises from the very moment in which you find yourself.

The *instinctive self* is always personal. It touches your own person directly. You remain yourself. You do not act someone else or represent anything outside yourself. Your own personal impulses are at work. Whatever entity you are at the moment, there is no need to specify or define who you are. You are the *instinctive self,* the impulse that is exposed, alert, sensitive.

Often, once you are touched physically your emotions come into play. The way we use language reflects this reality. You may say, "The beauty of the sunset was very touching." Or, "The music touched my heart," or, "It was such a touching moment!" Being touched by an image or a sound or a smell affects you like physical contact.

The spontaneous reaction of the *instinctive self* is not concerned with results. Actions, or reactions, are not to be understood, justified, or explained. Because you need not plan or structure your reactions, you are free of pressure to accomplish a specific result. All your actions are, in effect, reactions.

The intensity with which your energy springs to life corresponds to the intensity with which you are touched. Your response may be delicate or violent, light or ponderous, for it is only a reaction to its stimulus. As if you are an infant, everything touches you, for everything is new. The aroma of a good meal will continue to elicit a response regardless of how often you smell it, for you react out of a recurring need for food.

This work cannot be approached from the outside—you cannot assume a limp, wear a fake nose, sit in a favorite chair, or stroke some personal object in order to calculate or create the correct reaction to this exercise. The external manifestation of your inner state will be the shape your body takes, the definition of your gestures, or the degree of brightness of your eyes. As you plunge deeply into your *instinctive self* in this course of study, you declare war against your capacity to reason and your learned responses. As an actor, you don't need to perform to any external expectations that might exist.

These exercises, unlike the ones in the previous chapter, will be impossible to execute alone. You must work at least with one partner. Partners provide the sensory stimulation allowing you to connect to your center as completely as possible. If you touch or caress a partner it will be neither to express compassion for your mate nor to derive pleasure from the gesture but because of an impulse that has touched your center.

Be involved totally with your own center, disregarding what your fellow actors may be doing if you're working with a group. Create your own space and live within it. Concentrate totally on your own actions.

Suppress nothing. Keep yourself completely open. Allow the body to react in a natural, spontaneous way.

No words are to be used. If the voice needs release, it emerges from the body unrestrained, unforced.

Each session consists of two parts:

- Tuning In: Exercising the instincts.
- Triggering: Setting off instinctive reactions through the physical stimulation of our senses.

The Tuning In exercises for the *instinctive self* are very different from those for the *vulnerable self.* They are much more purely physical. The Triggering segment then quiets the body, centering the mind so the actor is completely open and free to respond to physical stimulation of the senses.

There are four model sessions provided here—one each for touch, hearing, sight, and smell. You don't work on the sense of taste because everything it can offer the actor is covered by the work on the sense of smell. The senses should be explored in the order given. Therefore, the *instinctive self* work will last at least four sessions, but any or all may be repeated as often as desired.

THE INSTINCTIVE SELF:
FIRST MODEL SESSION—TOUCH

Tuning In

All the exercises that follow should be used in each session. Each run and freeze segment should only last a couple of minutes. Altogether, the Tuning In exercises should take about fifteen or twenty minutes.

Run-Freeze. Work individually, ignoring any other actors, except to avoid physical contact. Run about the room, freeing your body, loosening your arms, legs, chest, neck, hips, toes, jaw muscles. Free your voice as well—through sighing, shouting, or spontaneous vocalization. Freeze all at once. You are absolutely immobile. Even your eyes are motionless. Not even your breathing betrays the life within you. You are frozen in time—beyond time. Stay this way until your impulse leads you to run freely again. Then freeze, and proceed as before.

While you run it is important not to think about the position you will take when you freeze. Stop in mid-movement, in whatever attitude you happen to find yourself. Run and freeze over and over until the next exercise.

Run-Sit-Freeze. This exercise is performed just like the previous one, except that you drop to a sitting position and then freeze. As before, maintain absolute immobility in whatever position you land in, until your impulse liberates you to run and sit again. Without planning it, try to vary your sitting position each time.

Run-Lie-Freeze. This takes the exercise one step farther. Here you fall to the floor, lying in the position your body assumes spontaneously. As before, without conscious thought, lie each time in a different position.

Run-Sit-Lie-Freeze Combination. It is up to you to assume as wide a range of frozen attitudes as you can, always with the proviso that they are free and unpremeditated.

If you are working with a group, the following four exercises will expand your instinctive responses.

Zig Zag Echoes. Form two lines, with a designated leader standing near the "Initiator" (Actor #1 in the diagram on p. 42). On the instructor's signal, the Initiator emits a vocal sound. Any kind of noise will do—loud or soft, pleasant or harsh, just as long as words are not used. Actor #2, facing the Initiator, picks up the sound, not trying to imitate it, not thinking about it, merely echoing it instinctively and passes it on, as in the diagram, to Actor #3, who echoes it and so on to the end of the line.

The leader may wait until everyone has echoed the sound, or may signal the Initiator to create a new sound, once the first has been

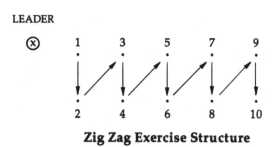

Zig Zag Exercise Structure

passed to Actor #2. In this situation you are all constantly at work and always alertly focused on your "shoulder" to pick up and pass along the sound. The leader may signal the Initiator to continue indefinitely in this manner.

Body Zig Zag.   This is the same exercise, only on the group leader's signal, the Initiator creates a physical movement without sound, freezing in the final attitude of the movement. The Initiator makes no attempt to give the movement literal meaning. This movement is echoed in zig-zag fashion as before. The movement should be in staccato and not in slow motion, since slow motion is a reasoned action and never the kind of spontaneous movement you want in this exercise.

Combination Voice/Body Zig Zag.   At the leader's signal, the Initiator makes a vocal sound and a body movement simultaneously, and you follow the same procedure as earlier.

The Motor.   Stand in a circle about four feet apart from each other, with one actor, the Initiator or "Motor," in the center. Neutralize yourself physically and emotionally so that you can absorb the Motor's actions and rhythms. Not trying to make any specific sense, the Motor immediately begins a series of repeated patterns of vocal sound and physical movement, which he or she sustains. Watch and listen in the circle until you are filled with the Motor's actions and your own body and voice want to respond with activity of your own. Once the feeling in you completely takes over, one by one, break the circle, walk into the center and join the Motor, responding instinctively in whatever manner feels right to you.

There are no rules to obey. As long as you don't make sense or try to be clever, as long as you follow your impulses, your only guide is what you have taken from the Motor. Your responsive action doesn't have to mimic the Motor or react in unison with his or her sounds or movements unless it seems right and natural for you to do so.

Don't deliberately create a unity with the Motor, but if it happens without design, continue within it, moving freely. All movement should spring from your inner self. If a discernible pattern emerges eventually, it will be a consequence of the unity you share with the other actors and the Motor.

The action continues until the leader decides to select another actor to become the new Motor and everyone else combines in a new circle to repeat the process.

The time it takes for each actor to become motivated enough to join the Motor in the center of the circle will vary from actor to actor and from exercise to exercise. It is important not to force a reaction. If the motivation is not genuine, it is better to wait until the impulse is stronger before participating.

After you've done all the Tuning In work, choose a partner with whom to work and begin the Triggering exercises.

Triggering: Stimulating Instinctive Reactions

It may be helpful to spend several sessions on *touch* before moving on to *hearing* and then in turn to *sight and smell.* Since you will be transforming all your senses into touch and connecting directly with your absorption center—your midriff, right under your solar plexus—start to practice with the sense of touch itself. Close your eyes so that you may concentrate only on touch. Your midriff should be bare. And you must start in as pure a state of rest or neutrality as possible.

Neutrality.　To achieve neutrality, stand erect and tight, holding the breath. Then slowly, keeping your erect position, exhale and relax the muscular tension in your body. Repeat this several times, after which stand without moving and without tension for a moment or two to reach a state of inner neutrality. Then move on to the next step.

The Balloon.　In one quick breath, inhale deeply, filling each part of the body, inflating it like a balloon—arms spread, chest expanded, legs open, up on the toes. Hold the air for a moment, then all at once release your breath and let your body collapse to the floor, allowing it to fall whichever way it drops. Inhale again, inflating yourself to a standing position before collapsing again. Repeat this several times, then remain collapsed on the floor in a state of rest, without any need to act. You will remain motionless until you are stimulated by your your touch instincts into movement.

Focus.   Turn your attention to the area of your body between your solar plexus and your belly button. I call this area the midriff but it is alternately referred to as the gut or the center. Focus awareness there without tension. Feel the area develop increased sensitivity. It should become an alert entity.

   If you are working with a partner, one of you should initiate the action so the other becomes Activated. Then reverse the roles of Initiator and Activated.

Touching 1.   When you have focused all your energy on your bare midriff, the Initiator goes and quietly touches you below the solar plexus with a variety of objects, pleasant and unpleasant: a tickling feather, a lightly pricking pin, a warm object, a cold one. React completely to the sensation in whatever impulsive way is natural. If the sensation is slight or more intense, the reaction should correspond. The Initiator must allow each reaction to happen before moving from one object to the next.

Touching 2.   Repeat what you've just done, but now you are touched on other parts of your body: the hands, feet, back of the knees, armpits, ears. While you are being touched, keep the concentration at the solar plexus so that every contact sinks directly to the central touch area, which creates the responses. In that way, whether the touches are pleasurable or uncomfortable, they connect immediately with the central sense.

Touching 3.   Open your eyes. Keeping all the focus on your central sense of touch, move about, touching a variety of objects with different parts of your body, allowing an instinctive reaction. The Initiator may startle you with noises, by creating stumbling blocks, flicking the lights, blowing cigarette smoke, and so on.

THE INSTINCTIVE SELF:
SECOND MODEL SESSION—HEARING

Tuning In

Repeat the exercises exactly as in the first session, spending about fifteen minutes on them. Then find a spot in the room and stand with your eyes closed.

Triggering: Stimulating Instinctive Reactions

Neutrality. As with the sense of touch, achieve neutrality, by inhaling and exhaling while tensing your body, then relaxing it.

The Balloon. Repeat this exercise as before, inflating and collapsing your body. After several times, remain in a prone position.

Focus. Again, repeat what you did with the sense of touch, focusing on your center, right below your solar plexus. Be silent and still until complete calm pervades the room.

Hearing 1. Your partner makes a non-vocal sound—rings a bell, raps the floor with a stick, blows a whistle, claps hands, stamps, or whatever. Whether the sound is strong or soft, it should hit you in the gut, through your focus on the central sensory area.

Hearing 2. After a moment, another non-vocal sound should be introduced and repeated. The type of sound and the intervals between sounds are left to the judgment of your partner. In this fashion, continue to react to the variety of sounds and rhythms in succession.

Hearing 3. Your partner may introduce vocal, non-verbal sounds at this stage: mewing, chuckling, whistling, spitting, and so on. You may react to meaningless syllables in a variety of pitches and degrees of intensity. Words, which may trigger the mind's interference, are to be avoided.

Hearing 4. Now your partner creates sounds with a variety of musical instruments. It is preferable that all sounds be produced live, but if snatches of recorded music are to be used for an effect that can't be created otherwise, they must be alternated with live non-musical sounds.

Always look for new responses in this study without knowing what kinds of sound stimuli to expect. Your partner will vary the timing of each new sound, and may add a series of sound patterns to cause a fresh reaction to a sound you have become accustomed to.

THE INSTINCTIVE SELF: THIRD MODEL SESSION—SIGHT

Tuning In

Go through the run-freeze exercises as described in the first session. Try all the group exercises as well, if applicable to your situation. Spend a quarter of an hour Tuning In.

Triggering: Stimulating Instinctive Reactions

You and a partner should take positions about two feet apart facing each other after deciding who will be the Initiator and who will be the Activated.

Neutrality.   The Activated partner stands in neutral, attained as in the previous sessions, with eyes closed. Then, instead of going into The Balloon exercise, precede directly to concentrating on your midriff as the Initiator stands motionless.

Focus.   Become aware of your center, below your solar plexus, and without any tension make it feel alive and alert. When your midriff has attained the height of its sensitivity start the first exercise.

Sight 1.   When you are the one to be Activated, you open your eyes. Whatever you see—ceiling, lights, partner—you should try to see as if for the first time. Allow the sights to be absorbed directly into your center, your gut, your midriff, and let the body react freely without forcing a response.

Sight 2. Now the Initiator goes through a series of movements for the benefit of the partner, but without making physical contact. As the activated actor, react to each of the Initiator's movements instinctively: a gentle, flowing movement might evoke a tender impulse; a sudden staccato movement such as a rapid, bird-like waving of hands could startle or create hostility.

The Initiator should try to stimulate a wide spectrum of responses by making movements with varying rhythms, close to, as well as far from, the activated partner. The Initiator can grimace and make any sort of bodily contortion that will provoke different reactions.

The Balloon. Do the exercise, inflating and deflating your body as described previously, ending up on the floor with closed eyes in a state of rest.

Sight 3. Open your eyes and respond to the changes in mood created as your partner varies the lighting. Your partner may continue to play with the lights, even using strobe, projections, and other light sources. Remember that all responses should be immediate and unforced. All reactions should come from the gut.

THE INSTINCTIVE SELF: FOURTH MODEL SESSION—SMELL & SENSORY COMBINATION

Tuning In

Take the fifteen minutes or so required to go through all the run-freeze exercises just as you did for the first three sessions.

Triggering: Stimulating Instinctive Reactions

Find a spot in the room to work. Stand on your feet with eyes closed.

Neutrality. Achieve neutrality through breath and release as you've done before.

The Balloon. Do the Balloon exercise as described above, and end in a collapsed, prone position on the floor.

Focus. Turn your attention to your midriff and focus awareness there in a relaxed way, without forcing or tension. Feel your midriff develop increased sensitivity. It should become an alert entity.

Smell 1.   After your partner has given you the time to focus, he or she should introduce a variety of odors, one by one, giving you ample time to absorb them and react. The odors may be pleasant and un-pleasant—perfume, ammonia, food, an old shoe, a rose.

Sensory Combination 1.   You should redo a Balloon exercise and end in a prone position. Then your partner should introduce a variety of stimuli to your senses—touch, hearing, sight, smell—in any manner that will occasion an instinctive response. Avoid planning or structuring your reactions. Keep the spontaneity of what you experienced in your physical and emotional memory.

LOOKING BACK

Now that you've experienced your *instinctive self,* you will be able to draw on it for the stage. When you are working on a scene, you will allow your instincts as the character to be available to react sponta-neously to whatever happens within the situation. Therefore, your character's reactions will always be true.

Moreover, you will know how to use spontaneity as required. How? Let's suppose you've been rehearsing a role for four weeks, or even longer. You have gone over every nuance of the part, over and over, yet you must appear onstage as if this were the first time. So you call upon your reflexes, the muscle memory you learned here, and you become sparkling fresh, not only to the audience but to yourself.

With the next self, you will learn to mask the qualities you discovered in your *instinctive self.*

4

The Social Self

The *social self* is the part of you that controls your instincts and emotions. It is as if you are two persons at the same time, the repressed *instinctive self* and the *social self* who watches the outside world and behaves according to its rules. You create an image to fulfill demands made upon you by society.

The spontaneity and innocence which are so marked in the *instinctive self* are buried deep in the controlled, wary *social self.* The *social self* recognizes, focuses on, and suppresses emotions which are "inappropriate" to a given situation. A salesclerk may be insulted by a customer; an employee may be intimidated by a boss; a student may want to explode into laughter at a teacher's mistake. But in these and other analogous situations, self-interest (ambition, fear, embarrassment) or kindness (concern for the feelings of others) requires that you do not react openly.

Usually the eyes and the face reflect your inner state. You can read feelings on a face, and the eyes reveal the depth of these feelings. In the *social self,* the facial expression will be one to conceal rather than reveal the inner state.

There is a conscious need to conceal and you are aware of how you attempt this concealment. To conform to what is expected of you, you may have to adopt expressions and manners you do not feel.

The social self is the first of the aspects of the self that will make you aware as an actor of your expressive tools. Through the practice of the *social self* you discover how to use the varied possibilities of your body and your voice. Unlike the *instinctive self* when you are never aware of what might develop out of your instinctive reaction, the *social self* deliberately selects the outer expression, the form, behavior, and manner in which you express one emotion and feel a different one. In a word, you put on a performance.

The *social self* teaches you to plan your behavior and act with precision, creating with exactness what you want to communicate when you assume the feelings of the character you are to portray.

The *social self* appears to function in complete freedom, yet in extreme instances you may be in virtual slavery. Take the case of the "corporate wife." Married to an "organization man," she smiles sweetly when she entertains his business friends, refrains from involving herself in causes the corporation frowns on, serenely packs up her children and her household when the corporation transfers her husband to another city or country, no matter how often this happens. Her own identity and concerns are subordinated to her husband's career. She must deny the anguish she feels from losing her identity, giving up friendships, and putting down new roots over and over again. She becomes the actress in her own life, living her *social self*.

Understanding the *social self* is the key to understanding a character's complexity.

THE SOCIAL SELF EXERCISES

Each session of work on the *social self* should be divided into two parts—before you can mask emotions, you should experience them in their "pure" form. So begin with a Tuning In exercise in which you select an emotion, concentrate on it, and let it take over your being, allowing it the utmost freedom. Then work on the contrasting or opposite emotion in the same way. Having experienced these diametrically opposed emotions you will have a better understanding of what you will be masking when you act out imaginary situations and circumstances.

You should set aside at least three sessions for work on the *social self*. During each session, don't try to explore more than three pairs of emotions. It is better, in fact, to realize one pair of opposite emotions fully than explore several pairs in a shallow manner. The only reason I offer you the opportunity to explore more than one pair per session is because there may be days where you just won't be able to feel certain emotions as much as others.

The following is a list of contrasting emotions:

- Cheerfulness/Melancholy
- Confidence/Fear
- Serenity/Anger
- Enthusiasm/Boredom
- Caution/Impetuosity
- Hope/Despair
- Compassion/Malevolence or Contempt
- Trust/Suspicion
- Bravery/Timidity

You may use these pairings or devise others that may be more resonant to you personally. During these Tuning In exercises, the total time spent on each pair should not exceed ten minutes. Over the course of several sessions however, you should explore as wide a range of these emotions as possible.

THE SOCIAL SELF: MODEL SESSION

Tuning In—Exploring Emotions Unmasked

As with all Tuning In exercises, find yourself a spot in your room or studio in which you have the space to work. Relax in any comfortable position, sitting or lying on the floor. Do not stand because it is important that you experience this exercise emotionally first and since there is some physical strain in standing, you could feel tense or obligated to move.

Start by selecting an "emotion"—I'll use cheerfulness, as the first example. While you remain relaxed, consciously create a "seed" or "spark" of whatever emotion from the preceding list that you want to work on, and implant it in your inner self. You may close your eyes if it helps you to visualize the exercise and intensifies the feeling for you.

Concentrate on that "seed," and will it to grow, so that cheerfulness slowly begins to fill every part of you. The emotion should spread throughout your body, into every pore, muscle and cell. Then, when the feeling completely fills you and you feel as if your body can't contain the emotion, let it burst free and lead you into physical and vocal (wordless) action.

Let your body respond physically. Leap into the air, roll on the floor, turn cartwheels, jump for joy, kick your heels. Make any natural movement that your being demands, as long as the activity is unforced. You should feel that you are one with the emotion and its expression.

As you continue to express the emotion, the activity will increase the intensity of the feeling, which in turn will trigger new activities, creating a spiral of energy.

A moment or two after it has reached its peak and you have physically expended all the emotion you built up, relax briefly again. This time find the opposite emotion—in this case the antithesis to cheerfulness being melancholy. Now concentrate solely on melancholy as you did with cheerfulness, and go through the same procedure.

Let the feeling start as a tiny "seed" deep inside you. Once again, slowly feel it grow, watching it in your mind's eye as it steadily envelopes your whole being. When you can't remain stationary because the emotion overcomes you so completely, express it physically and vocally.

If you're working on your own and the first pair of emotions were fully experienced, you may want to forego attempting another pair so the feelings you've experienced remain sharper in your memory. If the first pair didn't connect fully, try one or two more. Then move on to the situation work that follows.

Exploring the Masking of Emotions

After you experience emotions and their contradictions, proceed to create situations based on what you worked on. In these situations, you should learn to deny what is inside you, inhibiting or suppressing your instincts and emotions to the point where they cannot rise to the surface. Your *social self* expresses feelings appropriate to a given situation, regardless of inner contradictions.

When I'm teaching my classes, I usually give all the actors the same situations and let them explore each individually. So even though everyone will be working on the same emotions everyone works alone. If you have a relationship within the situation, the other person is imaginary, as is the street you may walk down or the door you may open.

So put on your social mask. Take as much time as you need to develop your own situations fully. If you're working on your own, read through each of my sample situations first, and then begin to act out the circumstances as fully as possible. If you'd rather work on a different pair of emotions where your response was stronger, then do so, creating an appropriate situation for that pair.

If you're working with a group, take turns being the leader, and inventing these situations for your fellow group members to work on. After you've tried my examples, make up your own situations for subsequent sessions.

Cheerfulness and Its Mask.   You feel so good you could dance in the street—you've just been promoted to the position you've been working toward for years. Now you and your longtime lover can finally afford to get married and have the kind of apartment you want. And to top off everything your beloved's father—a miserable old man who hated you before he even set eyes on you—has just died unexpectedly.

Of course, if your partner ever discovered how you really feel about the old man your wedding might be off. So you go to your darling's house, bursting with the news about your job, and find the family with faces down to the ground. So what can you do? You pull your face down as well and shake hands and say, "There, there. At least he didn't suffer." You never crack a smile but you almost choke on the lies you're dishing out.

Melancholy and Its Mask.   Your classmates are having a riotous party before your graduation the next week. You are too embarrassed to tell everyone you'll have to repeat a course and won't graduate with them.

You feel like hell, but you don't want to be a drag. A party like this doesn't need a wet blanket. So you live it up and let them think you're going to continue to be one of the gang when they graduate, although you know they will move on without you.

There are any number of ways actors approach these situations. In one of my workshops, an actor began the first situation above by dancing in the street to express his jubilation. He then put on a mask of grief suddenly as he knocked on the door. The effect was hilarious. From time to time during the exercise he let a happy grin break through on his face, then pulled himself together, making his lugubrious expression, when he resumed it, even more effective. Every now and then he would forget and give a joyous little hop when his mask of commiseration would slip.

Then there was the student who began this same situation by opening the door and walking in on the imaginary family already wearing his mask of grief. His profound sadness made one wonder if there was any emotion being masked at all.

A true complexity of emotion should engender some feeling of tension. If there was any inner struggle going on within this actor, I was not aware of it.

In these exercises you are meant to deal with conflicting emotions in such a way that the audience perceives the underlying feeling which is stifled but creates an intense force that acts on the character's behavior.

As with the first, there are an infinite number of ways of exploring each of these situations. I remember being particularly impressed by a student once who enacted the second situation by making her happy, "party" mask completely believable and fun. But anyone watching her couldn't help but notice that she had developed an intense physical mannerism—she was constantly yanking down the hem of her sweater. This small physical movement, however, perfectly expressed her inner tension.

In this first half of Exploring the Masking of Emotions, the examples dealt with situations that were created from the feelings that had just been explored in the preceding Tuning In exercise. In the second set of examples you, as the actor, inhabit the situations fully first and then discover the emotions and feelings as they arise out of the given circumstances.

Below, I've provided two examples of these situations. You

should feel free to create your own. The only requirements of the circumstances are that they must somehow place the actor in an imaginary public position forcing him or her to hide the true inner feelings bubbling below the surface.

The Waiter.   Imagine you are a waiter at a formal restaurant where personal impassivity is a requirement. You are to betray no reaction to anything you see or hear at the tables. Then one day, a physically stunning diner—the fulfillment of every romantic fantasy you've harbored since you were a young teenager—sits down at one of your tables. You eagerly go to take this beautiful customer's order hoping the diner's companion isn't a spouse.

As you pour champagne, you cannot help but be aware that this gorgeous creature is coming on to you. Moreover, as you lean over to serve the meal, the diner keeps making eyes at you and exhibits considerable charm. You have a strong suspicion that this is not accidental and are turned on instantly. However, you know that neither the diner's escort nor the maitre d' would appreciate any expression of admiration, let alone a more physical response to this come-on.

The Politician.   You are running for election and about to make the most important speech of your career. You have been trying for some time to locate a bathroom and find an opportunity to use it, and the matter is becoming increasingly urgent. But this is the only time you have to meet a number of persons vital to your campaign, and every minute spent with them could be crucial. Just when you feel the call of nature is too imperative to ignore, you are summoned to the podium before a crowd of thousands and must commence your talk.

Often when I conduct my classes I will bring one student forward who will then start acting out a basic situation. Then the group begins to chime in with variations to see what effect each suggestion causes. So one actor may call out, "You're in a movie theatre and laughing harder than you've ever laughed before." Another will pitch in, "But someone keeps spilling popcorn on your lap." In this way the group creates a masking situation for their fellow actor and learns from watching the response.

LOOKING BACK

When conducting these classes I have often observed that my students are much more at ease in the second type of situation. Perhaps this is because these situations are less complex than those involving conflicting emotions that have been imposed. Instead, the emotional life evolves naturally from the given circumstances.

I've noticed that being in a situation where there aren't specific indications of what their feelings should be allows my student actors more openness and spontaneity. That doesn't mean the exploration isn't necessary; it does, however, suggest that trying to act a result, such as "happy" or "angry" or "depressed," may be difficult. An organic exploration like that which we experienced in this chapter, would certainly help achieve it.

When you work on the *trusting self* next, you will make a complete about-face, removing your social mask and becoming totally open and free.

5

The Trusting Self

The actor needs to learn to take action without strain or tension. Making contact with the forgotten child within, with your naively *trusting self,* is essential to this process. Finding and accepting your *trusting self* will reinforce your ability to overcome self-consciousness and inhibitions. The childlike playfulness that is released through exploring this facet of your personality will liberate your creativity.

What is it like, this *trusting self*? It is the all-trusting part of you that exists in a completely non-threatening world—the Garden of Eden before the serpent appeared. Your most salient quality here is the serenity that doesn't recognize conflict either within you or within your environment. You are in harmonious sensual abandon with all that surrounds you. If menace exists, you are unaware of it. Accordingly, you are not vulnerable. There is no need for defenses. You receive from the world and give instantly, without calculation or reservation. You celebrate every element that touches your trusting body. It is as if each square inch of your skin were caressed by sunlight or bathed by the sea. There is no checking or editing of your responses.

You are responsible to no one—not even to yourself. You live in the moment, in an unconscious, aimless freedom. Your intellect is dormant. Your will has no place in this state of unthinking. Devoid of intention and curiosity, you have a minimal attention span. You are intermittently attracted to motion, scents, and sounds, which never cease. Temperature affects you. You are in constant and unaware activity, like a leaf drifting in the breeze.

The *trusting self* is a dancer, almost constantly in motion, like a silk scarf floating in space. It is motion without inner propulsion. It has no "motor."

Without memory, without accumulating experience, your *trusting self* surrenders to every element, doing as *it* wills, unresisting, accepting. It is bare, exposed, and free.

The *trusting self* does not possess or create any specific design either in its mobility or inertia. It is as malleable as it needs to be.

Unlike the *instinctive self*, where the center of sensitivity is located in one area (the solar plexus), the *trusting self* has no single center. Each part of the body acts and reacts, whether in isolation or in harmony with the rest of the body, as if it had its own center.

Your *trusting self* is the most elusive and abstract of all the facets into which you will fragment yourself. It lacks the self-consciousness of the *vulnerable self*. If two characters, one dominated by the *instinctive self* and one by the *trusting self*, were standing under a cliff and a boulder thundered toward them, the *instinctive self* would respond by running away or seeking shelter; the *trusting self* would open its arms and embrace the danger. At the same time, it is completely ignorant of the games played by the *social self*. And yet, your *trusting self* is more than merely an absence of these other facets. It is the aspect of yourself that lives entirely in its physicality. Its fusion with the world is complete and joyous.

TRUSTING SELF EXERCISES

These exercises are similar to those in the previous chapter in that there are two parts. Once again, you begin by Tuning In, only this time the exercises are physical, urging you to surrender your body, loosening it up, moving it toward the development of weightlessness. You then enact the situations in an exploratory way, passively letting the circumstances act upon you.

Every actor should try all three situations that I've supplied here. If there isn't enough time to do them in one session, spend two or three sessions on the *trusting self*. And of course, you may always repeat the work you've done—you'll be a better actor for it. Just remember to do the Tuning In exercises first, at the start of each session.

THE TRUSTING SELF: MODEL SESSION

Tuning In: Surrendering the Body

In these exercises, you are to be completely free of muscular tension. Just let yourself go and enjoy the utter abandon of being without responsibility for anything and everything, of giving yourself over without resistance. The first two exercises can be performed on your own. Spend a couple minutes on the Trampoline and perhaps a few more than that on the Balloon. The Magnet, the third exercise, requires that each actor have a partner, and this may require up to ten minutes.

The Trampoline. Make your body completely loose, as if you didn't have any bones, any skeleton. Imagine the floor to be a trampoline and jump up and down. Land lightly on your feet. Feel yourself float back into the air as the trampoline bounces you upward.

The Balloon—Isolations. As you did in the Balloon exercises in the *instinctive self* section, fill your body with air, exhale, and fall to the ground. Now, however, maintain the position in which you fell. Inhale, sending all the air into one arm, turning it into a balloon in your mind. Allow the arm to rise, to float as if it were not attached to your body. Exhale at once and the arm falls like an empty balloon. Repeat the process with the other arm. Then try it with both arms, one leg, the other leg, both legs, arms and legs together, and in different combinations.

Then inflate the head and neck, letting them float and then collapse. Before you rise to your feet again, inflate the entire torso and all the limbs, so that every part of you tries to float upward, your only contact with the floor being through the buttocks.

The Magnet. You must do this exercise with a partner. To begin, move into a standing position, facing your partner, about five feet away. Stand relaxed, with feet apart.

One of you becomes the "Magnet," the other, the *trusting self,* or the Activated. The Magnet should always start with the chest and slowly move it toward the actor awaiting to be activated. As the Activated, you let yourself be drawn without will or resistance until you are glued to your partner, the Magnet, chest to chest.

The Magnet releases the "pull" by stepping back and breaking the imaginary connection holding you. The Magnet then steps forward again, this time "magnetizing" another part of the body—a shoulder, a hip, the back, a thigh—by moving it toward the corresponding part of the Activated's body. As the activated actor you respond by mirroring your partner's curve in your own body, letting yourself be drawn shoulder to shoulder, or elbow to elbow, or whatever, until you and your partner are glued together in a new position. The partner who is the Magnet should initiate a whole series of "pulls" before stopping and switching roles.

Let me make a clarification at this point. When I say you are "mirroring" the Magnet's movements I don't mean to imply that this exercise is anything like the "Mirror" that seems to be the staple of so many creative dramatic classes. I never allow that exercise in my class because there's no feeling or emotion in it. It's empty. In the Magnet exercise corresponding movements must be felt or sensed emotionally first. You don't just blindly copy the actor in front of you. All impulses come from your center.

The result is quite different. Time after time in my workshops, students grasp this technique easily and the movement just happens, as if by magic. Try it and you'll see.

I have also noticed that when actors go through these exercises successfully, when they relax their muscular tension completely, almost no energy is used—even when they fall to the ground or leap abruptly into the air.

Situations

In these situations that follow, don't try to plan. Just move, and react to the circumstances, taking whatever action that feels right. Go with the flow of the exercise. Remember that the imagination comes into play in order to compel the body to take action, in order to physicalize the situation. Don't just sit there and let your imagination go by.

If you're working on your own, read through each situation a few times until what is happening is clear. Then let the full imagining of the circumstances impel you to physicalization.

If you're working with a group, it is probably more helpful to have one person speak the situation aloud as the other group members immerse themselves in the circumstances.

The Rowboat.   You'll notice this first situation is very similar to the example *force of nature* in the introduction to the *vulnerable self.* Only instead of feeling terrified and vulnerable by the ocean storm that is tossing your lifeboat, here as the *trusting self,* you open yourself to the experience. Imagine and work out the following:

You are lying in a rowboat in the middle of the ocean, totally relaxed, as if unconscious. The sea is calm, gently rolling. Now a soft breeze comes, ruffling the surface and rocking the boat gently, your body rocking with it. The waves grow stronger, and the boat and your body are tossed and turned about, spun, lifted, and dropped madly, without design. Your body has no sense of danger. You are not concerned whether you are wet or dry, immobile or jerked about, in the boat or in the water.

The water gradually begins to calm and you find yourself in the same position in which you began—relaxed, indifferent to what you went through, still the same *trusting self.*

The Shower.   With the Shower remember to abandon yourself more to the sensation of the water than the circumstances. In other words, don't worry about taking the soap and washing under your armpits— what is most important are the feelings that the cascading water brings up, and the physicalization that arises out of those feelings. Here is a brief description:

You have had a strenuous work-out or put in a hard day's work and you come home and get in the shower. As the water pours all over your body, surrender to the sensation fully. Let the streams of water run down your face, across your back. Raise your arms to let it wash across your armpits and down your sides. Spread your toes as it splashes against your feet. Embrace the water, revel in it.

The Inner Song.   This last situation finally encourages you to trust your voice and physicalize your being through song. We are rarely more open to the world around us than when we feel so good we have no choice but to sing out. Imagine the following situation as fully as possible and add as much specific detail as you need:

You are lying completely relaxed in an open field, green grass dotted with flowers stretching from horizon to horizon. The sky is a soft, clear blue. The air is fresh and clean. A clean, sweet breeze ripples the grasses and the flower petals. Butterflies drift by. Small birds wheel and swoop overhead. The air is filled with their twitterings and with the low hum of insects rising from the earth.

The song of sky and earth saturates your senses and your own song grows inside you. Let the song fill you until you can no longer contain it. Free your voice to sing aloud wordlessly and let your body move according to the melody. Touch and be touched by everything that surrounds you.

LOOKING BACK

Actors respond in many ways to these situations—by singing, laughing, or whatever physical activity is natural to the individual actor. I don't want to be specific because listing ways students react in these situations may suggest that a specific result is called for. This would defeat the purpose of these exercises which is to allow you, as the actor, utter freedom to express yourself in your own way.

The experience of the abandonment you feel through your *trusting self* will help you to approach characterization with openness and confidence. The *unresolved self,* on which you will work next, lacks this openness and confidence. Instead it is filled with doubts and constant awareness of the dangers entailed in reaching a decision.

6

The Unresolved Self

The *unresolved self* leads the actor directly to the heart of drama. In this chapter you will learn to recognize the dramatic elements that are found in all good characters and plays. The work on the *unresolved self* will help you to create and build a dramatic tension physically, and to take full advantage of it, enhancing the excitement of the subsequent action.

The *unresolved self* lies in this same intermediate condition wherein the essence of drama is found. This facet of your personality lives during times of transition, in the passage between one action and the next, the suspenseful thread weaving your actions together.

Every good work expresses the dramatic elements of a character through the physical, psychological, and emotional transition from action to action, which the actor learns to recognize and use. When matters go according to expectations, there is no drama.

When you lose emotional or physical control, when you flounder between decisions, you live in drama. A man who is as stable as the pyramids of Egypt may have power and beauty, but not drama.

We live in disharmony. Consciously or otherwise, we must continuously consider and adjust our responses in order to maintain our equilibrium.

When a birch is in danger of being uprooted by merciless elements, you watch anxiously. Will it snap? Can it withstand the violence raging about it? The suspense is alternately thrilling, frightening, and certainly dramatic.

We are vulnerable to the whims of destiny. We lack complete control over our fate and therefore our knowledge that the time must come when we will snap and break makes for constant drama.

Very simply, we find ourselves constantly having to make decisions—whether to take the subway or the bus or to walk home in the rain; whether to buy a newspaper, and if so, which one; whether to move to another city; whether to go to the dentist. These are the times in which strategies are weighed and action contemplated, no matter how trivial or of surpassing importance.

Whether you pause in a casual reply to a question or evaluate an action that will alter the course of your life, these tensions exist. Dramatic tensions increase as deliberations are prolonged.

Like a boxer, all your calculating, weighing, measuring, assessing, and maneuvering conclude with action—in this case, the blow you aim at your opponent. However, as soon as you initiate this blow, your *unresolved self* ceases to exist, only to be reborn in the instant after the blow is struck and you resume preparation for the next punch. The excitement resides not in conquest or defeat but in the preparation for battle.

The tensions of the *unresolved self* are not measured in terms of length of the indecisiveness but by the quality of the struggle, and its ability to keep audiences involved. The *unresolved self* deals with all forms of tension. Tension may be expressed through comedy, pathos, lyricism, or tragedy, in whatever manner the situation requires. Although these tensions must reach their peak and culminate in decisive action, the *unresolved self* is concerned with these dramatic tensions, not the conclusions.

Once the result is clear, whatever the outcome, the questions are answered. The suspense is over. The dramatic moment is gone.

THE UNRESOLVED SELF EXERCISES

These sessions consist of the same two parts as the *trusting self* exercises. You begin with a Tuning In exercise that, however, is tailored to the specific demands of this chapter. These exercises should take approximately a half-hour to complete.

As for the situations, remember that you should always be yourself rather than another character. As you explore these scenarios, let your focus continuously shift, thereby translating the inner struggle, the indecision, into a physical expression.

The following Tuning In exercises require one or more partners. Try rounding up a partner for this session. The situations, on the other hand, may easily be explored by the single actor.

These situations are examples I've taken from my years of teaching. You don't have to do every one. If you do decide to explore them all, I wouldn't recommend exploring more than three situations in one session.

THE UNRESOLVED SELF: MODEL SESSION

Tuning In: Physical Indecision

These exercises will help you to physicalize the emotional condition of indecisiveness. The first expresses physically what it is like when you are torn by conflicting forces. You know where your center is, but you cannot control the forces which are upsetting your equilibrium. The last Tuning In exercise sensitizes each part of your body so that you no longer are certain where your center is. This creates a mistrust of taking action which is dependent on a strong sense of direction.

Remember that after each exercise, the participants should change roles with their partners.

Pulling. This work is to be executed by groups of at least three persons. You, the activated one, stand loosely, feet apart. One partner pulls you by any part of your body. Another partner, or partners, pull you in one direction, then another, tugging you by an arm or a leg, grasping you around the waist, or the head. The idea is to physicalize the inner turbulence you feel when faced by indecision.

Non-Contact Pulling. For this exercise, stand in the center of the room. From one corner, one partner calls to you, urging you to come. Another partner calls from another part of the room, urging you with just as much conviction to go there. If you can work in a larger group, have other partners urge you to move toward them. You will find that this barking, cacophony of voices will tug you emotionally in all different directions. Key into the feelings this chaotic situation occasions.

The Snail's Antennae.   For this exercise, you should choose one partner with whom to work. Then decide which of you will be the "Activated" and which of you will be the "Initiator."

When you are the Activated—or the "snail"—stand facing your partner the Initiator. Your legs should be comfortably apart and your body loose and relaxed. With a pencil or similar object, the Initiator starts by touching you in the center of the chest. Your chest retreats, first in a short, subtle staccato movement, which then becomes a slow-motion recoil. It is the same kind of movement a snail makes when one of its antenna is touched—the first reflex is a small, sudden retreat of its body, which then continues, seemingly without stopping.

As your recoil reaches its limit, and you have been allowed to react fully, the Initiator touches the center of your back between the shoulder blades, stopping the initial recoil and beginning a new, opposite movement, as you pull in and away from the contact.

The Initiator should repeat this series of central touches a few times, first the chest then between the shoulder blades and then the chest again. You, as the Activated, will find yourself moving forward and back, recoiling from each touch. As the exercise progresses, the Initiator should try varying the timing so the contact is always unexpected.

Then the Initiator should start touching you elsewhere—on the arm, the leg, the head, the side—harassing you so that you are in constant retreat, never relaxing totally. The visual effect of this exercise is quite stunning. I tell my students that the Initiators may think of themselves as sculptors, and the Activated actor as the sensitive clay. One slight touch on the front of the shoulder and it recoils; follow with a quick contact of the back of the knee and it moves forward. Soon the Activated's body is taking all sorts of interesting shapes, moving in a flowing, unpredictable way, as if weightless, as if in outer space.

Situations

These sample situations I've supplied below are all designed to call up physical behavior associated with the moments of indecision that lie at the heart of the *unresolved self*. The tension builds in these situations. Let it take over your being.

Don't forget that these situations need not be definitive—you should create, enhance, and broaden the circumstances, the reason you're being faced with each challenge.

Each situation's exploration should take a minimum of three or four minutes. More often, you will find that five to ten minutes are sufficient.

The Tightrope. Draw a chalk line on the floor from one end of the room to the other. You can lay down a piece of string if you're working on carpet. In any case, walk along the line imagining it to be a tightrope high above the ground. You have just left the security of one platform and have stepped tentatively into space to traverse the slender line that leads to the safety of the far platform. Take a step or two and pause, letting the reality of your situation sink in—the distance you are from the other platform, your height above the ground.

What will you do—move forward or back, advance, hesitate, retreat, or turn again. Will you teeter precariously, only to plunge to disaster? Will the wire snap under the strain of your weight?

The Weightlifter. You are a weightlifter about to participate in the most important competition of your life. You've been challenged to lift a weight that is one pound more than you have ever lifted before. Will you make it? Will you be able to win this match? You have only a few moments to get ready for the lift. You must warm-up and prepare yourself mentally and physically for the event.

The Carpenter. You are about to saw a strip of fragile wood. You've splintered dozens of other strips in the process, rendering them useless. The one before you is the last strip of its kind and vitally necessary for the completion of a beautiful piece of furniture. Take up the saw. Are you going to ruin this strip too? Place the saw on the wood, hesitate. Turn the wood. Is this a better side? What do you do?

The Pianist. You are backstage, getting ready to perform your first major recital. Unfortunately, earlier in the day you fell and hurt your hand—not badly, but there is some stiffness. You're not sure how it will play. What should you do? If you perform badly, the critics will savage you. You might be able to play creditably, but maybe not. If you cancel this recital, there will be expenses you will not be able to meet. And there's the advertising, and all those people in the audience. The concert manager tells you that you have three minutes. What do you do?

The Actor.   You are waiting in the wings for your entrance on opening night. You are really nervous. You have butterflies. Your mind has suddenly gone blank. The audience is settling in as the house lights dim. What are your first lines? When do you enter?

The Hunter.   You are out alone on a mountain when you spot a huge grizzly bear. It hasn't seen you hiding behind a large rock, but the bear is slowly drawing closer. You take aim with your rifle but hesitate. There was a tremendous avalanche in this area recently and a loud noise could set off another. Besides, if you miss, the bear could become enraged and attack you. If you wait, he might just amble on by. But if you wait too long. . . . What do you do?

LOOKING BACK

In all these situations, indecisiveness was expressed through action which related directly to the given situation. Whatever hesitation was present grew directly out of the circumstances. For instance, as you walked the tightrope you might have winced as the wire cut into your feet, or got dizzy from the height. As the weightlifter you might have flexed your muscles and wiped your sweaty palms before grasping the bar.

As no two boxers are identical, we are all different from each other in the ways we contemplate our prospective action and plan our strategies. The way you, individually, develop the *unresolved self* exposes the individuality of each character you portray.

The next chapter on the *decisive self* explores the opposite characteristics of the *unresolved self,* focusing on the moment of action, instead of the period before.

7

The Decisive Self

Your discoveries, through the work you have done on the previous aspects of the *self*, have given birth to a new and comprehensive awareness, creating the *decisive self*. The work on the *decisive self* concludes the first phase toward becoming an all-around actor.

If the *unresolved self* is one side of a metaphoric coin, the *decisive self* is the other. Where the *unresolved self* calculates, plans, weighs, sifts, and selects possibilities, the *decisive self* acts the resolution. It enables you to overcome indecision and make choices.

When the *decisive self* takes over, the dramatic tension of the *unresolved self* culminates in dramatic action. The dramatic tension—physical or psychological—is always emotional. Therefore, when you practice your *decisive self*, the physical release is an emotional release as well. The degree of release is equal to the degree of tension that was built up.

As the *decisive self*, you understand the requirements of the moment. You evaluate and distribute your energies. You determine how you act, when and where, and for how long. If there are to be rules, it is for you to make them. Your conscious and intuitive intelligences coordinate, interconnecting all your facilities to make a choice. Each choice implies risk.

This is not the first time you have taken risks. In the *vulnerable self* you dared to expose your flaws. In the *instinctive self* you dared to experience your primitive impulses. In the *trusting self* you committed yourself without defenses. Daring goes hand in hand with losing fear of exposing yourself. The greater the risk, the more courage you have to muster to act decisively.

THE DECISIVE SELF EXERCISES

You will notice that the model session that follows is very similar to the one in the preceding chapter—it is a natural extension of the lessons just learned. As previously, a session should consist of both Tuning In exercises and the acting out of imaginary situations.

Another similarity to the previous chapter's work is that the Tuning In work requires at least one partner for the Assertion exercise and several partners for the Focus exercise.

However, there are twice as many situations in this chapter: the first set consist of the same circumstances you explored in the *unresolved self*; the second set of scenarios are new and unrelated to those from the previous chapter. All these may be explored on your own. Since there are twice as many, it should take several sessions to complete them all.

THE DECISIVE SELF: MODEL SESSION

Tuning In: Developing Self-Assertion and Focus

The purpose of the first Tuning In exercise, Assertion, is to practice exercising your own will. It is necessary for the *decisive self* to act always in defiance of someone else's will, but defiance becomes part of knowing who you are and demonstrating that you possess a will of your own. The purpose of the second, or Focus, exercise is to develop your concentration and determination—two important attributes of the *decisive self.*

Assertion.   I also call this lesson the "I Am I, You Are You" exercise. You begin by standing comfortably, facing a partner, whom I once again will call the Initiator. You are the Activated actor.

The Initiator begins a vocal or physical action. Whatever your partner does, you react immediately in a contradictory way, denying and working against your tendency to do the same. If the Initiator sits, you stand. If the Initiator opens his or her mouth, you close yours. If your partner speaks softly, you speak rapidly. If your partner runs, weeps, sings, you walk or freeze, laugh, scream, stammer.

After several minutes you both switch roles and you take your turn as Initiator. If you find more than three or four minutes is necessary, take the time that you need.

Focus. The Focus work is really three variations on an exercise I call "Follow-the-Left." This exercise requires a group where everyone stands in a circle, and a designated leader stands in the center. The leader chooses a group member who should initiate a vocal sound and repeat it over and over, establishing a pattern. The actor immediately to the right picks up the sound and joins in unison. The next actor in the circle continues the sound, and so on, until everyone is making the same sound in unison.

The leader then indicates the next actor in the circle, lets say Actor #2, the person to the right of the one who initiated the original sound, and everyone continues as before, making the new sound. After a round or two, the leader may indicate the next person in the circle, Actor #3, without waiting for the circle of sound to be completed. After one or two new voices have been added, always in order, the leader may go on to Actors #4 and #5, and so on.

The individuals in the circle always repeat the sound that the actor to their immediate left makes, in unison, changing the sound as the sound on the left changes. The leader makes the changes more and more rapidly. Many sounds will be overlapping—the only one that should be focused on is that which emanates from the actor to your left.

The second variation is structured exactly the same way only instead of the voice, a physical gesture is made and repeated, without sounds. The third variation combines the body and voice.

Remember, you must always do only what the actor to your left does. You can't let yourself be distracted by what anyone else is doing. It is as if you are singing in harmony in one vocal range and cannot let yourself slip into the melody of another group.

Situations: From the Unresolved Self

In all the situations that you explore, make sure to go through an unresolved state to a resolved one, to the *decisive self*. Here, it is preferable to create a situation complete in itself, with a beginning, a middle, and an end. Make sure not to portray someone else, but to be yourself in the situation. It is you who are walking a "tightrope" high above the crowd, not some circus character.

Be sure you understand the entire situation perfectly before you move. Conceive it in your mind up to the point where you take action, supplying yourself with all the motivation necessary. From then on, live the situation.

Remember, each situation must culminate in decisive action, but act it spontaneously. In each instance, read the corresponding situation from the *unresolved self* exercises (pp. 67–8). Go through the hesitation and contemplation as before, but now conclude the preparation by taking decisive action.

The Weightlifter.   No matter how big the barbell seems, this time your preparation leads to a firm decision—to lift the weight. Conclude the exercise with the decisive action. Whether you succeed or not is another issue.

The Carpenter.   After a careful consideration of the task in front of you, this time you decide to make the cut in the wood.

The Pianist.   Now, after all your worries, you nevertheless leave the backstage area, seat yourself at the piano and strike the first note.

The Actor.   The houselights go out, the curtain and the stage lights go up and you step onto the stage.

The Hunter.   After you've considered all your options, make a decision to shoot the bear or not to shoot it.

Situations: Not from the Unresolved Self

All the situations below must culminate in decisive action as well. These are not, however, based on previous situations. They are sketches or outlines for a situation that you should take the time to flesh out and make personal. Create and imagine the circumstances as fully as possible before beginning to explore the situation. Do your work on your own, trying not to be distracted by your fellow group members if you're not working alone.

Walking. Your legs have been in casts for months, following an accident. Now the casts have been removed, and although there is still some pain, you have been advised to try to walk again. You are not sure you'll ever be able to walk, and you have been afraid to try lest you have your worst fears confirmed. You are alone and debating with yourself whether you should attempt it.

The Phone Call. You have been striving to obtain a role in a play. You have to call the agent, producer, or director, knowing that this telephone call may make it or break it for you as an actor.

The Confession. You are a young man trying to tell your feelings to the girl you've secretly been in love with for a long time. You've dreamed of this moment over and over, but now the opportunity to speak is at hand. You have never exposed your innermost emotions to anyone before, and you find that the words aren't coming out. You're tied up in knots. She will go out of your life if you don't let her know how you feel, and it's now or never.

The Rebel. You are the child of a very authoritarian parent who has been directing every aspect of your life from the moment you were born. For years you have been trying to find the guts to assert yourself. You have always been afraid to bring matters to a head, but now the parent is about to make a decision for you that will change the current of your life to a direction you do not wish to go. It is time for you to take a stand.

Firing a Friend. You are an employer, faced with a most unpleasant responsibility. For years you have been very close friends with one of your office staff. Now he is having marital problems that are affecting his work in areas crucial to the business. You have reached the painful conclusion that you must tell him he must go. This would be difficult at best, but it is doubly so at this time since you know how vulnerable he is now.

LOOKING BACK

The *decisive self* gives you courage. The *decisive self*, regardless of the danger involved, acts. It is the fighter throwing a left hook at his opponent, leaving himself open. It is the sculptor putting a chisel to the marble, knowing a wrong blow could shatter it. The *decisive self* is willing to stake all, refusing to pull back even when the last moment can hold as much foreboding of defeat as promise of triumph. The commitment is total.

I have always believed that one of the most important aspects of the above exercises is how, as an actor, you must find ways to challenge yourself and experiment, exploring situations in which you are not necessarily an expert. You can become all you want to become. As all facets of humanity are within you, remember that you have the ability to become the fighter, the dancer, the hunter, the lover.

LOOKING BACK AT
LOOKING IN: A SUMMARY

The *vulnerable self* is that aspect which distorts your true being when it is in conflict with society's values. The *instinctive self* and the *trusting self* are unaware of the *vulnerable self*. They are instinct without reason and exist only in the present. The *instinctive self* is conscious of various kinds of stimuli and reacts accordingly. The *trusting self* accepts all stimuli without differentiation.

The *social self* knows the *vulnerable self* exists and acts to mask or deny it. It recognizes the *instinctive* and *trusting selves* and suppresses their spontaneity. The *social self* does not permit the exposure of uncertainties of the *unresolved self*.

When the uncertainties break through the protective armor the *social self* has created, the *unresolved self* emerges to dominate.

As the *decisive self* takes over, the *unresolved self* retires into the background until it is called on again. Unlike these others, the *decisive self* acts the resolution freely and consciously.

Remember that no human being possesses one trait only, and the character's truth requires that at least a tinge of the other traits color the dominant one. However, where one aspect of a role overwhelmingly dominates, you will benefit greatly by working in depth on that dominant trait.

Going below the surface to explore basic emotions is vital for you as an actor. I have devised this approach specifically for theatrical purposes, to strengthen you as an actor and as a person. With this approach you will be able to tap your emotions as if they are an inexhaustible well of understanding and identification with a character.

Your goal as an actor is first and foremost to bring your character to life and make it believable. To do this you must identify with your character on an instinctive and feeling level of understanding. That understanding in the study of your own *selves* has shown you what to do in a way that no intellectual analysis can do. *Looking in*side yourself gives you the character's truth—the traits which make one unique and which keep the character's actions consistent with those traits. This is basic to all characterization and, therefore, to all acting.

Having experienced this Looking In study you have taken an enormous step in learning how to create a character through physicalization, and you are ready to go on to Looking Out. There you will deal with ways of transforming yourself physically into your character.

PART II

LOOKING OUT

8

Steps Toward Transformation

Looking Out will give you physical techniques to expand your expressive capabilities and to transform yourself into any character. It helps you to *be* the character, *act* and *react* as the character, and *create* as the actor.

For the time being, while you are involved with Looking Out, tuck away in the back of your mind everything you learned in Looking In. Here, you are not concerned with the *selves*.

The point of view in Looking Out is directly antithetical to that of Looking In. You are not concerned with how *you* feel about someone or something. Instead, the subjects of the study are *elements of nature, animals,* and *man-made objects* and you identify totally with each of these. You assume the subject's traits, to the point where you integrate with it. By becoming one with your subject, you take its qualities into yourself.

In the event you are working on a specific role, read through all the workshop examples or model sessions in each chapter for a comprehensive overview of what they are all about and then select the one(s) most appropriate to the character you will be portraying.

A typical Looking Out session is a full and complete cycle. It consists of three stages. The first two, *Tuning Up* and *Exploration of the Subject,* lead to the third, *Physicalization of a Character.*

TUNING UP

Many forms of physical and vocal warm-ups are practiced by actors around the world. Almost every actor develops his or her personal warm-up before going onstage. Yet injuries are common in the theater. Muscle and voice strains are considered to be normal consequences of performing.

And then there's the actors' concentration. Often, when actors come to class or rehearsal, and sometimes when onstage, they bring distractions from the outside world. But in order to focus on your study or your role, you need absolute concentration. You may do warm-ups and expect them to rid you of these distractions; perhaps you've found they often don't produce the required results.

Those of you who have been working actors may find that you can't control your voice the way you want, or that your breathing is off, or that your body isn't focusing the way it should. You are a step or more behind where you want to be, and it's difficult to catch up. The outside world's distractions are insistent and may prevail over your best endeavors. These problems are universal among performers.

Over the years I've been examining these twofold difficulties—physical injury and the inability to concentrate—not only as a teacher but as an actor and student myself. I have developed a series of exercises that enable actors to step into their role physically ready without needing to grope for concentration.

The Tuning Up exercises that you will find in Appendix 1 prepare your body and clear your mind of distractions and therefore begin every model session in Parts II and III. They evolve from what is natural to the body. All these exercises, done at an easy rate, should not take more than thirty or thirty-five minutes and are well worth the time. Properly executed, they will drastically reduce the number and severity of the injuries actors have come to expect as routine hazards of the profession. At the same time, the exercises will automatically eliminate distractions and focus you on your work.

Tuning Up consists of three steps: centering, release, and ignition.

Centering

Centering is the process of collecting your physical resources—breath, voice, and body—locating the center of each, and placing each where it belongs. Centering gives you a kind of neutrality.

The centering exercises should be practiced at the start of each session exactly as is described in the appendix, without varying the order in which they are given there. Centering is practiced the same way for *elements of nature, animals,* and *man-made objects.* Breath, voice, and body are each to be developed separately, after which you will work on all three in combination.

Breath Centering. Breathing is, of course, part of everything you do, whether it is concerned with the voice, the body, or both. You practice breathing not only to help rid yourself of unnecessary tensions and focus on the tasks at hand, but also to create a space within yourself to make your breathing as ample as possible.

Voice Centering. The ability to control your voice from its centers will allow you to summon it with maximum ease, variety, and effectiveness. Where are your vocal centers? There are six—the abdomen, the chest, the lower throat, the upper throat, the sinus cavity between the eyebrows, and the top of the head. Although these voice exercises will expand your vocal abilities, use them for *centering* only. They do not replace other exercises and techniques for vocal development.

Body Centering. It is obvious that each part of the body is where it belongs. From this viewpoint, each part is already centered. What you are concerned with in *body centering* is the collection of energy into its central source.

The source of energy is the solar plexus. The energy from this source is distributed to each and every part of the body as need arises. The energy is supplied to the degree that is called for. For example, more energy is supplied to the hand to pick up a glass of water than a thimble.

Release

Release is the letting go of unnecessary tensions. These exercises are designed to rid you of the tensions you bring with you from your life outside the theater, not those you create for theatrical purposes.

After you have centered your energies by placing your breath, voice, and body parts each in its source, the release you practice will be maximally effective. The degree of release relates directly to the degree of tension. Imagine yourself a tempest with the wind silently pushing up massive swells which crest and break noiselessly. The lack of sound intensifies the pressure. You are taut, waiting for the sound to erupt in volcanic fury and devastate the world. You dread being overwhelmed by the awesome force of the expected violence.

The greater the intensity, the greater the release. Release is the ocean's calm after the tempest, the peace after the thunder claps when the winds and the crashing waves are stilled. This release is not a type of relaxation which is dulling or soporific. It is instead an active relaxation. This release of tensions fills you with positive, creative energy.

Release is practiced the same way for *elements of nature, animals,* and *man-made objects.*

Breath Release.   Many actors have problems with breathing. Tension may cause hyperventilation, dizziness, a gasping for air, or a faintness due to a lack of oxygen. When the breath is blocked, the voice and body are in trouble as well. Releasing the breath held in its centers frees the actor from blocks and accordingly, enables you to utilize your energies instead of being overwhelmed by them.

Voice Release.   A residue of stress or anguish will remain within your make-up until your voice is freed. The ultimate expression of unrelieved pain is a silent cry, a cry rooted in the depth of your being. To vomit out the pain and cry together, you must vent them with your voice.

Breath release will automatically support voice release and enable the voice to express itself without restraint and without physical harm.

Body Release.   In order to achieve release for your total being and thereby function at optimal capacity as an actor, your body release is combined with breath and voice release.

Ignition

Ignition is preparation for the immediate next step in this process—Exploration of a subject. These exercises are designed to put you in the proper mood or frame of mind for the subject you've chosen to work on. It readies you to deal with its physical requirements, putting you in a calm state if you are to be a peaceful cloud, a ruminating cow, or an arm chair. If you've chosen more active subjects—a storm, a gibbering monkey, a food mixer—the exercises will put you in a more animated state.

Basic Breath Ignition.   These exercises are designed to give an actor alertness, vitality, and focus. It directs the flow of oxygen to specific parts of the body so that your entire structure is evenly suffused with energy.

Varying the rhythms in breathing patterns also increases energy. When you change from normal respiration to rapid, shallow breathing, for example, you give yourself a new rush of oxygen to invigorate your actions.

Only after you are warm do you accelerate the pace and force of the movement. Energy builds on energy, and not until flexibility and stamina are sufficient to sustain maximum demands should you impose these demands on your body.

These breathing exercises are followed by *voice ignition* and *body ignition* exercises. And as I mentioned earlier, the ignition work should lead directly into Exploration. At this point, it may be a good idea to glance through the exercises in Appendix 1 and acquaint yourself with the material there.

EXPLORATION OF A SUBJECT

The heart of Looking Out lies in the *Exploration* work. What do I mean by this word, "Exploration"?

I mean improvisation. However, the term "improvisation" is not used in this book except in this paragraph. Improvisation has unfortunate connotations for many actors. Improvisation should be spontaneous, free of memory and intellectualization, springing from your innermost creativity and employing all your faculties. But many actors, when called upon to improvise, feel a pressure to create, and that cripples spontaneity and forces intellectualization. Accordingly, Exploration will be used instead of "improvisation" because not only is it less inhibiting but it is also a truer description of the procedure.

Explorations are created on the spot from your imagination—they are not recreated from past associations. Still, since the past is part of you, memories may arise and be used—but you should not consciously try to dredge them up. Instead, rely entirely on your imagination.

When you begin each session, remain in whatever emotional state you find yourself. If you are feeling somewhat vulnerable, remain so. If you come elated or depressed, you are not required to feel otherwise. Keep the emotions that are natural to you. In Looking Out your real feelings express themselves through the subject and not in opposition to it. You are free of the stress sometimes engendered in Looking In when your natural emotions had to be converted to other feelings.

The actual Exploration begins with the selection of a subject. There are three different types of subjects to be explored in Looking Out—*elements of nature, animals,* and *man-made objects.* At least a half-dozen sessions should be spent on each.

There is no fancy technique to learn in order to do these Explorations. You simply lie on the floor and put yourself wholly into the subject of study—whether it be thunder, a caterpillar, or a toothbrush. You let their essence and character saturate your being until you can't help but move and physicalize your new state. (More detailed information follows in each subject's own chapter.) The subjects are the three large steps necessary for transforming yourself as an actor into a character.

Elements of Nature

The first step is the Exploration of *elements of nature,* some of the most effective exercises designed to teach you to *be* instead of to *show, exhibit,* or *perform.*

The elements are the first step toward transformation because when fusing with nature's forces, you acquire characteristics that no human-scaled being or object can have. By becoming one with an element you are as all-encompassing as the element itself. You break through the barriers of the pedestrian to soar to the heights of the epic. When these characteristics are integrated into your being, you are "larger than life."

Every actor must understand and deal with the terms "size," "theatricality," and "larger than life." Although "size" is used primarily in connection with classical plays, this quality is inherent in all superior material. "Size" is that factor created by the playwright to invest his or her characters with emotions and actions that rise above the banal, even when the play deals with life's daily realities.

"Size" doesn't necessarily mean large gestures or other broad expressions. It is the actor's personal power—the energy that emanates from the actor's inner force. It is your responsibility to find the inner force and to draw from it the external expression that will enable you to fulfill the vision of the playwright.

Over the centuries, the quality of size has been exemplified by such theatrical roles as Oedipus, Lady Macbeth, King Lear, Electra, Mack the Knife, or Hedda Gabler. Whatever there is in these great dramatic creations—whether positive or negative—their size is larger than is understood to be "normal" in human beings. We tend to think of their joys and sorrows as traits of madness, but this madness is consistent with their nature of intense passions, as vast and deep as an ocean. Their fury is a tornado, their loves like the sun. Their tenderness is as soft as snow, but through their veins runs the blood of all humanity.

In your subsequent performance of such roles, you will be able to share what you have gained from your experience of these Explorations of nature with your audience, elevating and inspiring them as you have been affected by these elements.

Animals

The second category for subject exploration is *animals*. I define *animals* to mean all living creatures that are not human. Through the exploration of an animal's character and essence—the *animalization* of your own person—you'll discover and experience everything that is human, minus the brain. The animal teaches you to use strength, relaxation, agility, sharpened senses, reflexes, and the instinct for survival—basic behavior without which there is no theater. Drama is inherent in spontaneous action, the unexpected physical movement—for which the animal is the best teacher.

Studying *animals* teaches you to act and react instinctively as someone other than yourself. This is a different goal from that of your work in the *instinctive self* when you sought to uncover your own deeply rooted instincts for maximum self-expression. Here the goal is to capture and experience the inner life of the particular animal you choose to become. Now when you become an animal, you must react with the animal's instincts. Those instincts you have in common will give you some clues. So will the instincts, impulses, and reflexes you acquire as you work.

An animal is a creature with which you can readily identify. Each has a recognizable shape. Each has senses similar to your own. Each breathes, needs food, sleep, shelter. In short, you can empathize with the animal because to a greater or lesser degree the tools of its existence are analogous to yours. You tend to be less neutral in your reactions to the animal you see or imagine than to the impersonal elements of nature. You watch an animal move and you know, if you observe it carefully, its mood and its motivation. You can tell if the animal is afraid, relaxed, bored, or restless, even whether it is hungry or sick.

The line is a subtle one between your behavior and that of the animal in similar conditions. When you assume the identity of the animal and react as the animal does, you react for yourself as well. Its anger is yours. Its panic or its friendliness is yours, too.

Man-Made Objects

This is the third category of subjects to be explored. Physicalizing objects created by a human being stretches your imagination as an actor, enriching your creativity, and reveals new dimensions of expression. Through becoming an object you will be in touch with the most intricate part of the human structure: the creative mind. This mind's creativity teaches you to turn words on a script's printed page into a living being, to make the intangible concrete.

Man-made objects are a completely personal creation into which you pour your own inner life. Because the object is inanimate, your imagination generates the illusion that the object is alive—you create a new species of "being." When your imagination fuses with that of the original creator of the object, you will be moved by what is revealed of that creative life, as well as your own. When the qualities with which you have invested the object have universality, you can deduce that this inner life is rich and substantial.

You can neither create nor dominate the *elements of nature*, nor can you truly enter *animal* forms. The stimulus to your creativity came from the elements and the animals themselves, and you let them work on you through your senses and emotions. In the *man-made objects* study, you initiate the stimulus for the first time. You call on your imagination in a new way to create what the object's feelings and activities would be if it had feelings and could act. You physicalize a new life, bringing to it all that you are capable of.

CONTRIBUTION

As in the *vulnerable self* exercises in Part I, I have students in my workshops undertake *Contribution* as part of this Exploration work. If you're working on your own, however, you may just have to skip this component of the study. You can always prepare a Contribution and share it informally with other actors or in another class. But in either case, your audience should be somewhat familiar with what you're doing in order to assist you.

Simply put, Contribution is the presentation of what you experienced in your Exploration. The Contribution develops your ability to select what you think is valid. It teaches you to retain, to shape, and to refine what you discover in rehearsal. It teaches that every rehearsal is another step in the progression toward what you want to express. And to express it in front of an audience—in this case, your fellow actors.

You take a few minutes to conceive and structure what you want to present. Choose all or a part of your Exploration. This is designed to be a genuine sharing of what you found there. Try to enact it as you experienced it, but do so in a structured way. Rules do not apply to your contribution except that the presentation must be based on what you experienced in the Exploration. You don't talk about it, you just do it. It is up to you to determine how and what to contribute.

As you observe your fellow actors' Contributions, one after the other, you will instinctively retain in your memory what you like, what suits your own nature as an actor. It automatically adapts to become part of you. You also learn that there are many ways to express the same concept. What is not suitable to your nature will be discarded by you, but you will profit by insights into other approaches.

It is not necessary for everyone to contribute in the same session. However, all actors should contribute their work equally, if not in this session, then later, not only to be fair but also because you all have something to learn from each other.

DISCUSSION/DEDUCTION

After the Contributions by the actors, a Discussion should follow. This serves as the opening of your consciousness and intellect to that which you have been doing previously only on an instinctive, emotional, and unthinking basis. Now you talk about everything in a sincere effort to articulate in a straight, unadorned, and undistorted fashion your own experience and impressions of your fellow actors' Contributions. These Discussions are extremely important. They help you to understand how to overcome difficulties you encountered during the process.

I start the Discussion asking the actors for phrases describing their experience in their own personal Exploration. Then, from this list, another list is created that consists of what I call *group clue words.* As each actor pitches in a few words describing his or her personal experience, the other actors add their words to the list. From this collection, you choose all the words that best summarize your Exploration. This new, personal, and individual list of clue words may consist of an actor's own words mixed with those of colleagues.

The words are then put into three forms, created by adding each word to the appropriate sentence: "I am . . ."; "I do . . ."; "I feel . . . ." The sentences thus formed are the basic analysis necessary to become a character.

Using the sentences as a guide, I create the Situations in which the actors can each explore their individual characters. Because many of you may not be working with a group, feel free to add your words to the sample group words I've provided for each model session. From this new, enlarged, and personalized list, create your own phrases.

Study what you've written down and imagine an appropriate Situation in which to test your physicalization.

PHYSICALIZATION OF A CHARACTER

No character grows out of limbo. No human being exists without a past. The qualities you acquired through the Exploration of the different subjects, coupled with the understanding you gained from your fellow actors' Contributions and the following Discussion/ Deduction, can then be applied to physicalizing a specific human being—creating a character.

Use the experience of this workshop up to now as the basis for a character's emotional and physical life. Don't lock yourself into "thinking" the character. Your behavior emerges from what you experienced. In other words, deal with the character's true nature.

Your character needs something to do and an environment in which to do it: a *situation*. The character you embody is a human being. You can find yourself in as wide a range of situations as exist in the human arena—take the situations in Part I as an example. They covered a wide range of experience. As the character, you can experience situations in which you find yourself at ease because they are compatible with your nature, or in which you are under tension because they are contrary. Whether the situations are *ideal* or in *conflict*, they must be specific and real to you if your character is to have reality.

The situations on which you work should be simple. They should trigger your feelings so that you can act instinctively in a story, a brief scene, even a sketchy outline. Whether the circumstances incline toward the comic or tragic is irrelevant. Allow your situation to take its own course.

9

Elements of Nature

The *elements of nature* study is the first step toward transforming yourself as an actor into a character. This study enables you not to *show* the character but to *be*, to *exist* as the character.

An element *is*. A storm does not rage. It exists. Rain does not weep. It exists. The sun does not smile. It exists. The rage, the tears, and the smile are our projections describing states of being which have been filtered through our own perceptions.

In this study, you abandon that sense of self which keeps you firmly in your individuality and apart from the elements. The elements from which you will select are those which suggest the motion of life in their rhythms: the ocean, the wind, the rain, the thunder. You lose yourself within the particular element, sensing the enormity of its energy and scale.

You can exert no control over nature. You may intellectually comprehend the way the earth's rotation affects the wind, how water is drawn up into the atmosphere and released as rain, and means by which the discharge of static electricity results in thunder. Nevertheless, volcanos erupt, tides rise and fall, tornados spin. Their rhythms, sounds, silences, and dynamics are not yours.

These forces are beyond your usual understanding and alien to your body. You may understand their dynamics with your intellect, but on deeper levels your humanity cannot relate to the elements except with awe and wonder. The elements have nothing in common with you in your experience as a person, in the emotions that make you human. They are vast and impersonal. You may even feel one with these elements, but you always know the emotions that give this sense of unity are yours, not theirs.

When you become an element you have complete freedom that cannot be experienced any other way. You have no obligation to be of a specific form, to move in a particular way, to make any prescribed sounds. You are free to be the element as you feel it, to do what the element would do, as you are impelled.

To be of maximum benefit to my classes, I always choose elements of nature that suggest the motion of life in their rhythms. I would not select a mountain, for instance, because it seems static to me.

In my workshops, I usually explore six different elements that I believe give the actors access to the entire spectrum of movement and mood for the stage: a cloud, fire, darkness, thunder, ocean, and a volcano. That doesn't mean an enormous range of emotions can't be uncovered by a group of different actors all exploring the same element of nature. Depending on the actor, a cloud may be fluffily playful or inexorably menacing. The same actor may even discover fire to be friendly one session and ragingly destructive the next. Your Exploration of darkness may reveal it to be cozy or nightmarish and suffocating.

It is up to each actor to make the most of his or her work on these elements. All actors must acquire a sense of "being," "freedom," or "size." If I don't believe one of my classes has gone as far as I would like, I keep on working with these elements or I suggest additional elements for further study.

The order in which the elements are studied is irrelevant. Each offers a different kind of experience to the actor.

I shall now take you step-by-step through the first of my sample workshops, or model sessions, so you'll understand in every detail how this process works and what you as a reader or individual actor can take from it. The subsequent sessions are written out as well, but not in quite as comprehensive a manner as the first. However, all the sessions in this chapter are structured exactly the same way— Tuning Up, Exploration, Contribution, Discussion/Deduction, and

Physicalization of a Character. Only the element to be worked on each session changes.

I use many student examples in the next several chapters. All their names have been changed, and their responses edited for clarity.

ELEMENTS OF NATURE:
FIRST MODEL SESSION—CLOUD

Tuning Up

As always in my workshops, the first step is Tuning Up the instrument. Take twenty-five or thirty minutes to complete all the breath, voice, and body exercises that can be found on pp. 201–14. Go through the three steps—centering, release, and ignition. Proceed through the voice ignition and body ignition using the subject of the upcoming Exploration, a cloud.

Exploration

After the body ignition, start the exercise by lying on the floor in the A position. You should be relaxed, your arms and legs opened so they extend from your body diagonally at about forty-five degree angles (see Figure 1, p. 206). Your palms should be turned up toward the ceiling.

The aim of all these Explorations is the same: total commitment to the integration of your being into the life of your subject, a life that is not your own. In this session you are going to work on a cloud. Let your imagination take over, surrendering your mind and your senses to your cloud.

Your brain's tendency is to translate an experience into words, to identify it, to categorize it, to make selections. This is a common practice. Avoid it. Don't *act* a cloud. This is conscious. Become the cloud. Don't recreate your impression of it. Let its rhythms be yours, carrying you without design or structure. What should happen will happen.

Summon all your faculties and focus on the cloud. Concentrate to where your personal consciousness almost vanishes and your entire being fuses with your cloud. All your energies should be channelled to each moment's action.

Avoid curiosity about the cloud and, indeed, about anything else. You have never known what you are exploring now. Sense memory has no function here. You are in undiscovered territory, utterly open—senses and body. Although your senses as a human being have nothing in common with the element, use them as a tool—exposed, alert, sharp. Commit yourself to being the cloud, totally. Whatever contact you have with the world is the direct mindless contact of an element that may be limitless in magnitude or without restraint in its unbounded energy.

When you are one with your subject, wait, submerged in it, until its impulses drive you to action. You may find yourself waiting for what seems an interminable time, but this should not trouble you. When the subject demands activity—and it will—go along with it. Follow your impulse to action. Whether the impulse moves you quickly or slowly, smoothly or jerkily, respond as it dictates—crawling, leaping into the air, rolling about, twitching, lurching, exploding —whatever. Use your muscles no more than is called for. You may break into violent physical activity such as you never before experienced. The element's energy sustains the movement, not your own. And an element's energy may be infinite.

You may want to make vocal sounds. Don't imitate. The sound must rise from your being as sound rises from the element itself—because it exists and demands release from its source, in a natural way, not forced, not suppressed.

If you find that during the Exploration your oneness with the cloud diminishes, this is not unusual. It is only natural that when you work for twenty to thirty minutes on a subject, at some point in the exercise you may become distracted—by other actors, the classroom, or if you're working at home, a doorbell or telephone ring. Don't panic. Just find your own method to concentrate and ease your way back into your Exploration until you've once again achieved total identification with your subject. Try to spend at least twenty minutes on your Exploration.

Contribution

After the Exploration, I give the actors in my class ten minutes in which to structure their experience as a cloud for presentation to the other actors. Because everyone was absorbed in his or her own activities, everyone was unaware of what other people were doing. If you're working on your own, try to do this anyway. It will help you learn to be selective, to edit your experience for performance.

The form doesn't matter. Just stick to what the experience of being a cloud felt like to you. Each Contribution should only be a few minutes long. In my workshops, I usually have several actors contribute a presentation to the group, which altogether takes about fifteen minutes.

For example, in one class, I had a student, whom I'll call Amy. When I asked for her cloud Contribution, she circled the room slowly, dreamily, extending her arms out to the side. Every now and then she broke into a waltz step. She swayed and bowed as if she were in a blissful trance. Then she'd spin and continue circling the room, weightlessly.

Another student whom I asked to present a Contribution—I'll call him Bill—stalked back and forth with his clenched fists tight to his thighs. He stopped from time to time and stood staring into space. When he resumed his pacing he would kick out, glaring.

Is what these actors did typical of being a cloud? There is no such thing as typical. The experience of the Exploration is intensely personal and there is no predicting how an individual will react to a subject.

Discussion/Deduction

For the next step, everyone in the group sits on the floor and talks over what it felt like being a cloud. Each actor must now try to use words to summarize for the group the essence of his or her experience.

It came as no surprise to anyone in Amy and Bill's class that these two actors had very different experiences. Amy volunteered that she loved being a cloud. She grew lighter and lighter until she found herself high in the air, above everyone. She danced with the breeze and let herself be tossed happily in the sky.

Bill's cloud experience wasn't so merry. He felt heavy and morose, hanging low in the air. Wanting to drop his burden of water, unable to, and being angry with everyone he came across in the sky or below, he kicked them out of his path.

If you're working in a group, you should find the same variety of response. After everyone has had a chance to express his or her cloud experience in words, all the actors should take turns offering one phrase or brief sentence that captures the essence of their own personal experience. If you're working by yourself, write down your short sentence and add it to the sample list I've provided below:

Sample Group Phrases

- A cloud has no center.
- It is always in harmony with its environment, complete, content.
- It is gloomy, morose.
- It is lazy, sleepy, flattering, smooth, dreaming.
- Never aggressive, the gently soothing cloud floats about, adjusting its form to suit any vagrant breeze.
- It lets itself be divided with neither protest nor struggle. If it splits, it splits; if it fades, it fades.
- It is threatening.
- It does not reach out, preferring to keep to itself.
- It has no sense of self-realization or ambition.
- Its intentions are never known until they are revealed in action. Its actions are never known until they occur.

After everyone has contributed a sentence or phrase of description, each actor now comes up with single words that best relate to his or her experience. The words are to be spontaneous, unpremeditated. They should come right from the source of your Exploration. Because the Exploration is deeply personal, don't be concerned whether the words which come to your mind are similar or contradictory to those of another actor.

Everyone in the group should then get a pencil and a pad of paper and write down each word that describes your own experience as it is mentioned. If you're working on your own, add any words that pop into your consciousness to the list below that one of my classes created:

Sample Group Clue Words

Wistful, dreamy, light, caressing, touching, sensuous, erotic, no-gravity, airy, blissful, serene, passive, fluid, open, voluptuous, languid, enveloping, penetrating, angry, patient, indifferent, merry, heavy, free, moody, soft, penetrable, parasitical, balanced, graceful, easy, sad, content, loving, flirtatious, melancholy, sluggish, gentle, relaxed, aimless, calm, ambivalent, transparent, feathery, playful, whimsical, magical, wondering, unmotivated, egoless, naive, innocent, constant, evermoving, eternal, everchanging, impressionable, childlike, vaporous, white, unthinking, cool, morose.

For those actors working individually, choose all the words from the above list that relate to your personal experience of being a cloud. Some of the words on the composite list, obviously, may suggest to you ideas or distinctions that your experience didn't warrant. Regardless of the interpretations others may give the words, you are to be concerned only with what they mean to you. Write down your own list of individual clue words.

My students Amy and Bill, who revealed very different experiences in the Discussion, nevertheless chose a common word, "unthinking." The word obviously carries different connotations as well as a different tone for each actor. Otherwise, their word lists are evidence of their different Explorations. For example, Amy included words like "dreamy," "sensuous," and "playful." Bill chose "moody," "sluggish," and "penetrating."

Once you've chosen your words and formed a personal list, notice how some words from the above list describe conditions or states of being—"penetrable," "innocent," or "fluid." Others describe moods—"serene," "passive," or "aimless." Then again, other words, although presented as adjectives, imply action. "Flirtatious" suggests the act of flirting; "playful" implies the act of playing.

Now you must break your list down into these three categories by using them to complete the following sentences: "I AM _____"; "I FEEL _____"; and "I DO _____." If a word can fit into more than one category, select the one that brings it closest in meaning to what *you* experienced.

For example, Amy came up with the following three sentences: "I AM . . . light, dreamy, airy, fluid, open, graceful, aimless, feathery, magical, vaporous. I FEEL . . . sensuous, free, soft. I DO . . . flirt, play."

Bill broke his list into the following sentences: "I AM . . . moody, thoughtless. I FEEL . . . sluggish, unmotivated. I DO . . . penetrate."

Your Exploration will have led to your own personal set of clue words and subsequent sentences. This then forms the basis of your personal analysis of your experience as the subject—a cloud. This breakdown indicates the qualities which make up your specific cloud character. The next step is to create and work on a situation to fit the feelings and mood of this character.

Physicalizing a Character

Don't stop to think about this next step, but allow it to develop spontaneously as you go on working.

Each character is different because the qualities in each list are different, but each expresses *cloud* for the actor who experienced what his or her individual clue words and breakdown described. What is needed now are situations to fit the feelings and mood of the character—an ideal situation and a conflicting situation.

I usually suggest ideas for situations in my workshops, but you may create your own. The aim is not to create an enjoyable little story or playlet but to see how you maintain the consistency of your character in an ideal situation in which you're in harmony with the circumstances as well as a situation wherein you have conflicts. It is up to you to fill in the situation and to give as much physical life as possible to your character.

You don't have to explain your character or situation. Use the environment and the events you create to motivate your actions. Remember, you maintain your cloud traits throughout your creative work.

In all situations, everything is imaginary, including other people, doors, scenery, props, whatever. However, if there should already be a chair or simple object like a stick, this may be used.

To give you an example, for Amy's ideal situation, I told her that she was walking on air: she was going to marry the love of her life. And that very night she was going to meet her fiancé's family for the first time and she had to get ready, put on her best dress, check herself out in the mirror. Then she had to enact the meeting.

When I gave her this situation, she used her cloud Exploration and Deduction to create her character. We watched as she radiantly opened an imaginary door to her lover's home. She floated over to the dinner table. She seemed barely to touch the floor as she caressed her imaginary fiancé. Amy, it was clear to see, had embodied the light-ness of a cloud.

Then, in order to test her grasp of her cloud character, I asked her to try a new situation, a situation in conflict. I asked Amy to imagine that the dinner was a nightmare—formal to the point of rigidity. All the family members were stiff and unbending, and they cross-examined her about her past as if they were trial lawyers grilling a murder suspect.

Although in this situation Amy was close to tears, she appeared very charming to the family, lightly flirtatious whenever the opportu-nity presented itself, and airy in the face of their overt hostility—all aspects of her cloud nature as described in her breakdown list.

When one of my students comes up with a very different list garnered from his or her unique, personal experience, I come up with different situations. Bill, for instance, would have an ideal situation all his own. I told him that the girl he had been dating for five years had just dumped him. She told him that he was not to come around anymore. Bill reacted furiously. He stomped over to her apartment, kicked at the door savagely, and retreated grumpily when forced to accept the inevitable. Inasmuch as his Deduction had revealed him to be a sulky, bad-tempered cloud, this behavior was consistent with his character.

In order to strengthen Bill's characterization, I then presented him with a situation in conflict. I told him that suddenly his girl said "yes" after a long, unsuccessful courtship. She even suggested that the two of them go on a vacation together to places he'd always wanted to visit. Money was no object— her father would give the trip to them as a gift.

When Bill's cloud character encountered such a situation it seemed as if he were in a dilemma. He was highly gratified on the one hand, but his basic sour nature kept breaking through as he prepared for a celebratory night on the town, even as he declared his happiness.

Before moving on to the next element, it may be a good idea to read over this first session. Because I discussed the first workshop in such detail, I am not going to go into every aspect of the following model sessions. Each sample workshop will provide the basic outline structure for each session, sample group words, and a couple exam-ples of individual Explorations, clue word lists, and situations. Use what is provided as a general guide.

ELEMENTS OF NATURE:
SECOND MODEL SESSION—FIRE

Tuning Up

The first step and one of the most important. Don't skip it. Turn to pp. 201–14 and spend twenty to thirty minutes on the exercises. Make sure to do all three parts—centering, release, and ignition. For the ignition exercises, tune yourself to be fire.

Exploration

Find a spot on the floor and lie down, relax, and move your limbs into the A position. Spend twenty to thirty minutes exploring fire. Don't analyze or ponder this element—*inhabit* fire.

Contribution

Take ten minutes to structure what you experienced as fire. Then take turns presenting your Contribution.

As with all these exercises, the variety of responses is overwhelming. One student's Contribution was particularly distinctive. She began by lying on her back in the A position and then began to twitch her hands and feet. After a moment, she rolled over and got on her hands and knees. She crawled over the floor in that position, first in a small circle, and then more quickly in wider and wider circles. Her face was murderous as she hissed and spat. She brushed up against a column in the studio and struck at it. She threw herself violently against it and caromed off, rolling over and over on the floor, finally coming to rest on her hands and knees again, hissing and clawing. Carol did all this at incredibly high speed and in an intense, staccato movement.

I asked another student to present his experience. Dan also began in the A position, but he then sprang lightly to his feet, leaped into the air, and started bouncing weightlessly. He flung his arms up and laughed as he continued to jump like a pogo stick, up and down, up and down. His movements were quick and abrupt, with much less of a staccato rhythm than Carol's.

Discussion/Deduction

During the Discussion for this class, I asked Carol what she had felt in her Exploration. "Hatred," she replied, "Pure hatred. I didn't know I had that much feeling in me. I *was* fire. I devoured everything and it wasn't enough. I hated what I destroyed and I hated what I couldn't reach. I could have devoured the world." Carol had no idea where such anger came from but it left her feeling so drained and tired she could hardly move.

I asked Dan if he had experienced anything like that. "No way," he said. "I was successful in becoming fire, but I was a happy little fire in a fireplace, and my arms were flames and my fingertips were sparks that went up the chimney. I had plenty to eat and I was safe and comfortable. It was fun to be a fire. I wanted to giggle and go snap, crackle, pop!"

It should be clear from these descriptions that a wide range of responses to these exercises is possible. Perhaps your Exploration was completely different. In any case, try to come up with a phrase that captures the essence of how you found fire. Here is a sample list of descriptive phrases for fire that I culled from one group:

Sample Group Phrases

- It has no defined pattern.
- It is not symmetrical and never repeats itself.
- Its body has the potential to become all arms.
- It is in a constant state of agitation, of palpitation.
- It talks, sings, chatters, screams.
- It is all-devouring, claiming everything with which it comes in contact.
- It constantly demands new material to survive.
- Its arms are innumerable and ever-changing.
- It keeps nothing but reaches out for more and more, reaching in only as it dies.

From this description, it should be clear that fire has many facets. Perhaps some of the phrases will enrich your characterization. The next step is to come up with a list of clue words. Remember that the words you and your fellow actors come up with should be spontaneous and related to your Exploration. A sample listing to which you may add your own follows:

Sample Group Clue Words

Uncontained, destroying, egocentric, mischievous, unpredictable, hungry, thirsty, ruthless, whipping, penetrating, powerful, nervous, frenetic, giddy, tickling, cunning, devouring, spreading, edgy, restless, uncentered, invincible, suicidal, quick, murderous, energetic, light, contorted, extreme, volatile, unfocused, unbalanced, weightless, uncontrolled, omnipotent, giggly, all-consuming, cruel, flickering, wild, irritated, explosive, diabolical, agitated.

Note that some of the words listed here are the same as those found in the previous cloud workshop: light, weightless, penetrating. However, in the overall context of such contrasting elements as cloud and fire, the words have colorations that give them completely different shades of meaning.

From this group's clue words, choose all those that pertained to your experience and break them down into the three forms of sentences. Carol's words were made into the following sentences: "I AM . . . uncontained, unpredictable, weightless, quick, extreme, volatile, unfocused, unbalanced, uncontrolled, wild. I FEEL . . . diabolic, thirsty, suicidal, murderous, irritated, invincible. I DO . . . spread in all directions, contort, devour."

Dan's breakdown exemplifies his own personal experience: "I AM . . . energetic, light, volatile, uncontrolled, quick. I FEEL . . . giddy, mischievous, ticklish. I DO . . . tickle, flicker, giggle."

Physicalization of a Character

Here you must enact both ideal and conflicting situations created with your imagination. If your experiences resembled Carol or Dan's, feel free to use their examples for yourself. Perhaps by tinkering with some of the circumstances, you'll be able to create an individualized situation that will both highlight the characteristic behavior of your "fire" as well as challenge its depth by confronting it with an uncharacteristic or conflicting situation.

For Carol I came up with an ideal situation suited to her interpretation of fire. I told her she was a scientist for NASA who has been warning her superiors that the space shuttle plans were flawed and dangerous. No one listened. For months she'd got increasingly irritable and agitated, almost to where she became violent.

Then on the day of the launch she saw the shuttle disintegrate in the sky, killing people she'd trained with and grown to love. I suggested that perhaps she'd want to kill those who refused to listen, or to kill herself. She's alone in her office and free to go berserk. She can do anything she wants—smash her computer, wreck her files, pound her fists on the wall.

For a conflicting scenario, I came up with a natural extension of this situation. I told her that she was being interviewed by the media concerning the shuttle catastrophe. Being loyal to NASA, and knowing that if the truth were told the entire program would be scrapped, she decides to keep the truth to herself. This conflict should feel as if it is strangling her as she tries to restrain herself, to remain calm and poised.

The sample situations I came up with for Dan were likewise derived from his breakdown list of sentences. As an ideal situation I suggested he was at an amusement park feeling light-headed and full of beans. He finds himself in a hall of mirrors and sees himself all distorted—perhaps he breaks into giggles. He moves from one mirror to the next. Everything seems hilarious and an uncontrollable giggling begins to overtake him.

To put his carefree spirit to the test, I devised a conflicting situation where he was to imagine being in a funeral parlor. Accompanying a friend, the service is for someone he doesn't know. The long faces all around seem to be hypocritically solemn. The situation seems grotesquely funny but it would be embarrassing to laugh, and an outburst would harm a valued friendship.

Test the physicalization that you've discovered in your Exploration and Contribution in situations that would be both ideal for your character as well as the worst possible scenario your character could imagine. Be tough on yourself by creating a situation that demands a lot from your fire character.

ELEMENTS OF NATURE:
THIRD MODEL SESSION—DARKNESS

Tuning Up

Turn to pp. 201–14 and start with the appropriate exercises. Spend twenty to thirty minutes tuning your instrument, doing all three kinds of exercises—centering, release, and ignition. When you get to the ignition, tune yourself to be darkness.

Exploration

Lie down comfortably and relax, your arms and legs extended, palms up, in the A position. Let yourself slowly become darkness. Feel what it's like, how it makes you feel. Let darkness take over your being until you *are* darkness. When the impulse to move is so overwhelming that you can't lie still any longer, move in whatever way your darkness expresses itself. Whether your darkness makes you yell or whisper, roll on the ground or run in slow motion, follow your impulses no matter how small.

Contribution

Take ten minutes to structure a presentation of what you experienced as darkness. If you're working in a group, try to have as many members present a Contribution as time permits. If the group is small, you may find there's enough time for everyone to make a presentation. Even without a group, try to come up with a short distillation of your Exploration experience.

Discussion/Deduction

After the Contributions have been presented, take turns summarizing the Exploration of darkness experience. As in the previous sessions, a variety of responses to the exercise invariably present themselves. In one of my classes working on darkness, I asked a student named Frank to discuss his Exploration. His account is a good example:

> As I lay on the floor I could feel myself growing bigger and bigger and bigger, until I filled the whole room. I got up and walked around noiselessly, stretching out my arms and leaning forward to cover everything beneath me. I had no feeling about whatever I passed over—trees or people or cars or houses—it was all the same to me. I was so much larger than everything else—what could it possibly matter what happened down there?
>
> I kept growing, and as I grew I became lighter and slower until my every movement was in slow motion. I had no need to hurry. My advance was powerful, inexorable. Nothing could stop me. I moved

on, invading every nook and cranny of the earth. After I covered the whole world I held out my arms like huge wings whose shadows were black, black, black. I was lord and master, and everything feared me. I loved it. I laughed and laughed with pleasure, quietly.

Frank's experience is notable for its detail and specificity. His feelings went through changes—at first his darkness character seemed impassive. Then it began to revel in its power. Another student of mine, Emily, experienced darkness in her own way. This is her description:

> It was fun to be darkness. I tiptoed around and then I jumped forward and landed on something—an orchard, a city, whatever. I crouched over, enveloping everything, laughing and laughing to see everybody afraid of me, running for the light. I caught up with some of them and sneaked ahead to where they were going and blocked them with my blackness. I laughed to see them turn and try to escape me. It amused me to chase them. I was annoyed when the sun rose and pushed me aside. So I said, "What the hell, my turn will come again later."

After your group spends a few minutes in general discussion, listening to each other's experiences, everyone should try to come up with a single phrase that captures the essence of what they experienced. I'll include a sample list here.

Sample Group Phrases

- Darkness possesses no motor to activate it.
- It appears from nowhere and disappears into nowhere.
- It is present and not present.
- It is without sound.
- Without intention, it dominates all it touches.
- It covers, envelopes, and penetrates everything.
- Nothing affects it or can stop it.
- It is more intense than serene in its effect on us, but the intensity is due to its lack of expression and to its all pervasiveness.

Everyone should then take out his or her pad and paper and write down all the words that describe his or her darkness character as each actor takes a turn coming up with spontaneous one-word descriptions. Remember, write down only those words that really describe an aspect of your Exploration. For those of you at home, feel free to add a few words of your own and add them to the following sample list of clue words.

Sample Group Clue Words

Calm, quiet, sneaky, vanishing, enveloping, caressing, penetrating, dominating, serene, light, heavy, choking, proud, threatening, humble, devious, fearful, bold, ruthless, pitiless, uncaring, purposeful, intense, smooth, full, pregnant, swelling, protective, mysterious, plotting, warm, cold, peaceful, driving, humming, alone, great, invincible, crawling, still, careful, cautious.

To give you an idea of how personal this process should be, think back to Frank and Emily's description of their darkness characters. In many ways they were similar. But they chose lists of words that only had one word in common—"enveloping."

Otherwise, their lists were completely different. Frank chose the following words: calm, powerful, heavy, full, swelling, enveloping, mysterious, humming, alone, still. Emily's list included these words: sneaky, penetrating, smooth, light, vanishing, enveloping, purposeful, dominating.

After you've chosen your list, break them down into the three types of sentences as in previous chapters. For example, Frank broke his list into these three sentences: "I AM . . . heavy, full, mysterious, still. I FEEL . . . calm, powerful, alone. I DO . . . swell, envelope, hum."

Emily, on the other hand, divided her list this way: "I AM . . . sneaky, smooth, powerful. I FEEL . . . light. I DO . . . penetrate, dominate, vanish, envelope."

Physicalization of a Character

Now that you have your guide to your darkness character, read over the sentences a few times. Then create a situation that would have all the ideal circumstances for your darkness character to thrive. Imagine it fully enough to try acting it out. Then come up with a situation that would put your character in deep conflict.

To give you a further idea of what I mean, here is the situation I suggested to Frank. Because he seemed to be so overcome with the thrill of power, I told him that he was the head of the FBI and was calling a meeting to plan a campaign against subversives—a new group of radicals who are plotting to overthrow the United States government. I suggested he take his time and present his arguments forcefully, reveling in the prospect of squashing all opposition, haranguing any staff member who seemed to hesitate in this effort.

Then, to test his characterization of darkness I told him to now imagine that the president has bowed to public pressure and is forcing him, as head of the FBI, to make an apology on national television for being over-zealous and trampling on the rights of American citizens. He could protest, argue, and be resentful, but he must obey.

Emily's ideal situation would be one which would highlight her fun tormenting people. I proposed a situation where she don a hideous-looking Halloween costume and then go outside and hide behind a bush. Every time a group of little kids came by she could jump out, yell "Boo" and scare them, make them drop their trick-or-treat baskets. After she'd tried that situation I suggested a conflicting one wherein she's doing the same thing, only the next group that comes by are a couple of large, scary looking, rough men carrying switchblades. She sees that they're looking for victims to rob and who knows what else. They spot her and she starts to run but keeps tripping over her costume.

I'm sure you can come up with situations closer to your Exploration's experience in which you can practice being your darkness character. Make them as personal as possible.

ELEMENTS OF NATURE:
FOURTH MODEL SESSION—THUNDER

Tuning Up

Start by tuning up your instrument. Turn to pp. 201–14 for the specific centering, release, and ignition exercises, tuning your breath, voice and body in each category. The ignition exercises should tune you to be thunder. After approximately a half-hour of these exercises you will be ready to explore.

Exploration

Lie on the floor in a comfortable A position. Relax and let your tensions drain away. Then slowly focus your whole being on thunder.

Put yourself inside this element, letting yourself become thunder. When your body is completely filled with this element, when you've merged yourself into the essence of thunder, let your impulses to move or vocalize take over. Don't worry about how long it takes to get to this point. When it happens, let it happen. Spend at least twenty to thirty minutes exploring your thunder character.

Contribution

After you've fully explored your element, take a few minutes to come up with a presentation version. Remember, don't make up a story, just distill your experience into its essential components. After several or all of the group members have presented their Contributions—whatever time permits—move on to the next step.

Discussion/Deduction

Now you should take the time to talk about your experiences as thunder. This particular element often causes extreme reactions because of its very nature. Anger is a common response, though the means and methods by which different actors express their rage varies according to their temperament. Amy had a typical Exploration which she described during the ensuing Discussion.

> As I lay on the floor, I could feel anger building up in me. I rolled over and over, and when I hit the wall I exploded. I pounded my fists on the floor and I screamed. I leaned against the wall, completely worn out, all my energy used up, and as I rested, the anger came back and grew and grew until I was choking.
>
> I screamed. I jumped high, and jumped again and again and again. I ran around and around. I felt the energy in me growing and when I released it in a scream this time it gave me more energy. As I continued to run and scream, the energy increased. My bursts of screaming were unpredictable and uncontrollable and I felt vital, strong, elated.

Bill's experience was different. As you are supposed to, he tried to block out everyone in the group and concentrate on his own Exploration. But Bill found himself so "full of rage" that he became "tremendously aware" of his fellow actors. The way he resolved this problem is interesting:

I hated them. I wanted to punch in their faces or stomp them flat. The only way I could keep from releasing my violence on them was to yell until my throat hurt or to bang my fists against a column. Some part of me realized that I must not hurt anyone, so I ran and screamed and yelled, getting more and more angry, fiercer and fiercer. I was afraid I wouldn't be able to control myself, but the outbursts of screaming relieved the pressure, and I went on, running and yelling.

Now, I realize that I had come to class feeling upset about something that had happened at home. Becoming thunder concentrated all my feelings and intensified them until I let them burst out of me.

It's important to reiterate that you must not let yourself lose control to the point where you do damage to yourself or other actors. There is a very fine line between being spontaneous and moving freely, and letting loose and being out of control completely. Bill's experience should also make clear how important the Tuning Up exercises are. You will be using your body and voice in a very charged and physical way. Don't try it without being properly warmed up.

After the general discussion, take turns contributing one phrase that describes the experience. Altogether these phrases offer a more complex and deeper characterization of thunder than yours alone. The following are what one of my classes came up with:

Sample Group Phrases

- Blind, sees nothing.
- Hears only its own voice.
- Is born at one end of the universe and dies at the other.
- Frustrated to the point of insanity.
- Will destroy all that stands in its way.
- It splits its environment in two, separates the world, totally concerned with its own fury.
- Born in fury, dies in fury.

These phrases should be useful in broadening your own feelings about what a thunder character may be like. Then take turns pitching out one-word descriptions of your experience. If you're working on your own, add your words to the bottom of this list:

Sample Group Clue Words

Unpredictable, consuming, choked, sublime, dark purple, black, careless, untouchable, shadowy, vengeful, piercing, grumbling, screaming, uninhibited, hilarious, spontaneous, energetic, magnifying, senseless, superior, metamorphic, changing, regenerating, red, all-powerful, god-like, exasperated, hurt, violent, menacing, pounding, forceful, strong, immense, passionate, king, boss, in charge, loud, staccato, incessant, sharp, devouring, destroying, unrelenting, screaming, quick, abrupt, controlling, murderous, torturing, explosive, hot, fired-up, furious, roaring.

From your personal list of clue words, break them down into the three sentences: I AM . . . ; I FEEL . . . ; and I DO. . . . Read them over a few times—your sentences are your guide to your thunder character.

Physicalization of a Character

Now it's time to create some situations in which to explore your character of thunder. Bill and Amy broke down their personal lists and I suggested possible situations for them from the sentences they created. Amy's sentences were: "I AM . . . dark purple, untouchable. I FEEL . . . choked, senseless, exasperated, hurt, violent. I DO . . . grumble, pound, menace."

The ideal situation I thought up for her character was simple. I told her that she was a graduate teaching assistant at a university and that she should enact a confrontation with a professor who has just given her thesis a failing grade. He made no comments about the work itself, he failed her out of personal animosity. This imaginary confrontation, I thought, would allow Amy to express the rage of her thunder's character directly.

To put the same character in conflict, I proposed the same circumstances with one difference. Instead of confronting him, she decides to go home. She opens her door only to walk into a surprise birthday party given to her by her colleagues. There's a pile of beautiful gifts and, by a quick look around the apartment, it's clear no expense has been spared. Amy's thunder character should feel a good measure of conflict as she smiles and thanks her friends, while all she really wants to do is kick a wall.

Bill's choice of words were very similar and the sentences he came up with were as follows: "I AM . . . unpredictable, uninhibited,

energetic, red, loud, staccato, quick, abrupt. I FEEL . . . careless, hilarious, strong, passionate, hot, fired-up. I DO . . . consume, pierce,
scream." For an ideal situation for his character, I suggested that he has
been drinking in a bar, getting loud and obnoxious, when someone
blows smoke in his face. There is nothing he can't stand as much as
smoke from a cheap cigar. Very quickly there's a confrontation which
escalates into a brawl.

To put Bill's character in a situation more alien to its dominant
nature, I created a different variation. Once again, I suggested he
place himself in a bar where he's getting progressively more drunk
and belligerent. He starts to pick a fight with one man, but this guy
backs off and apologizes. He turns to another man and says something insulting, but this fellow agrees with him. He keeps trying to
find someone who'll start some trouble, but everyone humors him.

ELEMENTS OF NATURE:
FIFTH MODEL SESSION—OCEAN

Tuning Up

Warm up with the Tuning Up exercises on pp. 201–14. Take your time
and go through each centering, release, and ignition exercise, Tuning
Up to this session's element of nature—the ocean.

Exploration

Once again find your spot in the room in which to work and lie down
in the A position. Close your eyes and focus on the ocean, letting its
rhythms, its size, its essence take over your body and emotions. Don't
worry about how long it takes—it will happen. Then when you must,
let yourself become the ocean, moving into action, physicalizing your
impulses. After twenty to thirty minutes of exploration, stop and
prepare your Contribution.

Contribution

Take ten minutes to structure and distill your Exploration into a presentation that shouldn't last more than a few minutes. If you're working in a group, limit the Contributions to fifteen minutes in total.

Discussion/Deduction

As in the previous sessions, discuss your experiences in depth after you've watched your fellow actors' Contributions. Keep an ear open for responses to the ocean Exploration that were different from yours, as well as to descriptions that may give your perception of ocean a deeper, richer meaning. Perhaps your response was similar to Dan's. He related the following experience:

> I sat up, with my body undulating. Back and forth, back and forth. I seemed to be swaying, rocking like that for I don't know how long, when suddenly, without volition, I was on my feet. I felt huge. My head and arms had their own energy and went in their own directions, flowing, jerking, undulating, snapping. My legs moved of their own accord. Whatever my parts did, I was content. My breathing was loud. Even though everything was going in different directions I felt centered—enormously centered, enormously powerful. My strength was immense.

From this description it should be obvious that Dan's Exploration was very physical and contained a lot of movement. What is particularly interesting is that Dan reported that "no matter how violent or extreme my movements, I felt no muscular strain; I used little energy." This is not unusual to hear from my students. The reason Dan's movement seemed so effortless is because he was truly letting the element of nature serve as an energy source. Of course it felt as if he weren't working hard.

Carol, another student, shared a similar experience. Though she started on the floor it wasn't long before Carol, as she told us, "became so suffused with energy that [she] couldn't contain" herself. She described the rest of her Exploration,

> My arms lifted and undulated. I lay there with my body joining in the swaying. I writhed, every muscle lithe and sensuous. I was female, fertile, omnipotent. I rolled on the floor to rhythms deep inside me. Rolling, I pushed obstructions aside, splashed against the shore, tossed spray into the air, and moved constantly without rest or need for rest.

Carol's energy seemed boundless and full of life. Like Dan's, it was full of movement and physicality, but a physicality that was generated from the "rhythms deep inside" her body. Obviously, it was a very organic, connected Exploration.

After you've talked about your experiences in a similar manner, take turns trying to boil down your perceptions of the Exploration into one sentence. These are the phrases one class came up with:

Sample Group Phrases

- A force that relies on nothing but itself, sure of itself.
- Selects its time for action as it sees fit.
- Repels all it dislikes, generous to what it likes.
- Paternal, constantly watchful.
- Beyond question.
- Constantly challenging the world around it.

Perhaps these sentences will remind you of an aspect of your ocean Exploration that you forgot. Altogether, your group's phrases should create a well-rounded and rich characterization of the ocean.

The next deductive step is coming up with a list of clue words. Go around the group and call out one-word descriptions of your ocean Exploration. Everyone should write down every word that describes his or her connection to the exercise, thereby creating an individual list of clue words. These are some that one of my classes came up with:

Sample Group Clue Words

Greedy, proud, springing, tickling, omnipotent, mysterious, aimless, goalless, peaceful, conclusive, crushing, primal, no muscle, no focus, no direction, penetrating, spitting, splashing, explosive, fun, destructive, undulating, sexy, fluid, heavy, flowing, forever, spineless, spasmodic, lethargic, silly, dizzy, cranky, surprising, inconsistent, timeless, maternal, sensuous, unpredictable, uncontrolled, formless, shapeless, enormous, sloppy, expansive, thick, eternal, massive, hallucinating, ever-changing, unaware, tension-free, release, birth, womblike, rolling, uninhibited, dancing, singing, violent, turbulent, beating, cyclical, calling out, merging, enveloping, reaching out, kicking, raging, languorous, bottomless, constantly in motion, chuckling, dynamic, moody, restful, unperturbed, containing, lovely, wet.

If you're working on your own, add whatever comes to your mind to this list and then read through and write down each clue word that you feel appropriately characterizes an aspect of your Exploration. Then break them into the three types of sentences that we've been working with.

For example, Dan broke down his individual list of clue words into these three sentences: "I AM . . . omnipotent, timeless, enormous, unperturbed, without muscle; I FEEL . . . proud, peaceful, expansive, restful, centered; I DO . . . spit, splash, explode, undulate." This should serve Dan well as a key into his ocean character.

Carol made the following breakdown sentences: "I AM . . . primal, free, fun, wet; I FEEL . . . fluid, sensuous, languorous; I DO . . . flow, dance, shake, splash, envelope, undulate."

Physicalization of a Character

Working from Dan and Carol's characterizations, I came up with some situations which they could explore as "ocean." As an ideal set of circumstances for Dan, I suggested that he was an artist, filled with a great surge of inspiration. He's been given an important commission to paint whatever he wants. He's prepared a large quantity of paint and is ready to splash it onto the huge canvas.

Then as a conflicting situation, I proposed a slight change to the above scenario. Instead of a commission to paint anything he wants, Dan must create an advertising design for the manufacturer of a new type of dog food. The concept that the ad company came up with is awful. He loathes the entire concept—and the project itself. But he must paint it anyway.

I told Carol that she was a belly dancer, undulating and shimmying for a group of friends who were all responding enthusiastically. I suggested she should concentrate on feeling the joy of movement, the vitality and sensuousness in every muscle.

To put her expansive ocean character in a more challenging situation, I then told her to do the same thing, only this time at a sales convention. The all-male audience gets progressively rowdier and more drunk. She must try to ignore the lewd remarks and avoid the hands trying to paw her or tuck bills into her costume.

When you create your own situations, don't hesitate to try several variations on the same general circumstance. The more situations into which you place a character, the fuller and richer the characterization will become.

ELEMENTS OF NATURE:
SIXTH MODEL SESSION—VOLCANO

Tuning Up

As always, start with the body, voice, and breathing exercises that can be found on pp. 201–14. Take your time going through all three steps—centering, release, and ignition. When you get to the voice and body ignitions, tune up for your volcano Exploration.

Exploration

Now move to your own space on the floor and lie comfortably in the A position. Close your eyes, relax any tensions still lingering after the Tuning Up work. Then slowly bring yourself to the study of a volcano. Let its essence seep into your center and gradually take over your very being. When you become one with the volcano, follow your impulses to movement and to vocalization. Explore this element of nature for twenty to thirty minutes.

Contribution

After your Exploration spend about ten minutes on your own, devising and structuring a presentation that reaches to the heart of your experience. It should only be a few minutes in length. Then spend a quarter hour or so taking turns presenting your Contribution.

By this sixth and last session, everyone should have had a turn presenting a Contribution. Perhaps if your group is small enough, you've been able to do a number of Contributions for your group.

Discussion/Deduction

Now is the time to sit and talk about your experiences. Take turns describing your Exploration of a volcano. If you're working on your own, you should now have six written descriptions of your work on six elements. Don't throw them away—they may just come in handy, reminding you of the important work you've done.

As you describe your volcano Exploration you should notice that this element, in all likelihood, has brought out very strong reactions. Read what Emily experienced:

> I sat up and wrapped my arms around my legs, hard and tight—brooding, heavy. I was feeling rage piling up inside me. I rumbled deep in my center. Suddenly, I heard a long, sustained scream coming from my mouth. As my body exploded, tearing loose in spasmodic activity, I was the lava, spurting out in an uncontained burst of energy. I spun, twirled, tumbled, fell, destroying everything, burying it. As the lava kept pouring out, I was out of control, gigantic, swelling. Gradually, my physical activity lessened, but not the intensity of my rage. It was still boiling inside and I knew it would burst out again. I was restless and tense, waiting for it to tear loose again and destroy.

Emily's response to the exercise, as intense as it was, is nothing unusual. Her Exploration, however, does have a good example of how the voice suddenly, impulsively, is used. She describes the scream surging from her subconscious as if she were hearing someone else. This is another indication of how well she had integrated her own being with that of the subject.

Frank's response was also a very intense one. At first, he said he felt "the lava was building up inside" him. Unlike Emily's volcano, Frank couldn't scream and release his tension.

> The lava was filling every cavity in my body. It was hot and nauseating. I wanted to vomit it out, but I couldn't. It was stuck inside, gagging me. It was hard to breathe. My body became tense and it ached. I could feel the lava bubbling and seething, pressing to find an outlet. I shook. I felt myself jerking spasmodically, tenser and tenser. I pounded my stomach and ribs, hoping to release what was inside me, but nothing came out. I finally sat down, twitching with spasms, choking, waiting for the lava to burst free.

I hope it is clear from all the student examples I've provided that there is no "right" result to be reached during an Exploration. Whether your volcano destroys villages, or sits smoldering, all that matters is that the choice comes from your center and your total identification with the subject. Don't think about what your volcano should be like; let what happens happen.

Now, you should try to reduce what you've described, or written down, into one phrase or sentence. These are some one of my classes thought of:

Sample Group Phrases

- A volcano is absolutely centered.
- It is a loner, a world unto itself, neither wanting nor needing companionship.
- It is never in harmony with its environment.
- Evil-hearted, it seeks to destroy, to bury; when it cannot, it is frustrated.
- Even at rest, it always frowns suspiciously.
- It can never achieve serenity. In action it is violent, vomiting; in quiescence, constipated.

From these sentences, my students' ideas and feelings about their own personal volcano broaden and deepen. The next step, as you should be aware by now, is the sharing of clue words. As the group suggests one-word distillations of each of their volcano experiences, write down any words that describe your Exploration. For those of you on your own, here's a sample list:

Sample Group Clue Words

Contorted, spontaneous, son-of-a-bitch, daring, tall, quiet, frustrating, eruptive, emotional, sparking, searching, passionate, fear, superior, birth, fantastic, indiscriminate, intense, isolated, destroying, virile, schizophrenic, pleasurable, contained, with a lid on, anxious, turmoil, paranoid, volatile, monumental, still, terrorizing, self-destructive, gigantic, uncontained, alive, daring, hot, rumbling, oozing, violent, fuming, boiling, suppressed, releasing, conflict, hating, fury, remote, anger, irrational, dynamic, smoldering, crescendo, against everything alive, authoritative, uncontrollable, pervasive, constipated, flaring, vindictive, reactionary, terrifying, bone-breaking, brooding, expelling, isolated, bursting, inner, lower, intense, pelvic, spouting, abominable, fierce, sporadic, threatening, heavy.

These words should provide you with a number of choices from which to form your own personal list. The next step of Deduction is turning the words into the breakdown sentences. Emily broke her words into these sentences: "I AM . . . uncontrollable, fierce, indiscriminate, volatile, intense, irrational; I FEEL . . . vindictive, violent, furious; I DO . . . terrify, flare, burst, smolder, spout, erupt, destroy, rumble, fume."

Frank's sentences resulted in the following breakdown: "I AM . . . pervasive, reactionary, sporadic, intense, contained, with a lid on; I FEEL . . . pelvic, sexual, inner, heavy, brooding, fearful, anxious, in turmoil, suppressed, frustrated, paranoid; I DO threaten, frown, self-destruct, boil, bury, jerk, contort."

Physicalization of a Character

Now comes the time to test out the characterizations in imaginary circumstances. For Emily's volcano, I suggested she enact a situation wherein she has a boss that she really despises. For years he's done thousands of stupid things and blamed them on her while taking credit for anything good she produced. Suddenly, she gets a great offer of another job and can afford to finally tell off her boss. She gets to work early and waits in his office for the big confrontation. A few moments later, he walks in.

You can try this situation or make up one of your own based on your character's breakdown. Remember the first situation should be an ideal one for the character, a scenario in which the character will most easily express its dominant features. The second situation you should explore, is the opposite. For Emily, I suggested that she's still working for this boss that she hates. Every time she thinks of how he has taken advantage of her, she could almost choke on the feelings that boil up inside her. But now, with all the credit cards filled, and loans to pay off, she must go to him, smile, and calmly demand a raise in salary.

Because Frank's Exploration resulted in such a conflicted character, the ideal situation, ironically enough, would be a situation in conflict. I proposed a scenario wherein he'd just discovered proof that his wife was being disloyal. He confronts her. His two children are in the adjoining room. They are happily playing and he wouldn't want to cause them anguish by losing his temper.

A situation that would test Frank's volcano characterization would be the opposite. Something like having a wife who confronts him with the evidence of his cheating and disloyalty but she doesn't rant and rave. Instead, she's facing him, forgiving him, offering love and support.

ELEMENTS OF NATURE:
REVIEW SESSION—COMBINATION

In this last session (though this doesn't have to be the last—feel free to do this combination workshop more than once), review each element you dealt with in previous workshops. You should do this *before* you go on to the next category of subjects, *animals*. This session is abbreviated in some ways—there's no Contribution or Discussion/ Deduction. However, there's most certainly a Tuning Up.

Tuning Up

Do the exercises as you have been throughout the chapter. When you get to the voice ignitions, however, try the exercises with a variety of subjects from the *elements of nature*. Since the focus of this session is a combination, don't limit yourself to just one, or even two ignition exercises.

Exploration

Starting in the A position you should relax and begin your Exploration on any of the elements that you've previously encountered. Remember, you've been a cloud, fire, darkness, thunder, the ocean, and a volcano. Now, be any element you feel like being. You may choose to stay with it or become another element—or every element, as long as it evolves naturally.

After twenty or thirty minutes, as I said before, skip the Contribution and Discussion/Deduction and go directly to the work on the situation.

Physicalization of a Character

Create a simple situation. Get out of bed in the morning, bathe, brush your teeth, or whatever you do when you wake up. Get ready to leave the house for work. Do this first as a character based on one of the elements. You could start as a cloud character, then a fire character in the same situation, and go down the list. The order isn't important. After this, create other situations, either ideal or in conflict, in which you may be as many element characters as you wish.

After you've had your fill of *elements of nature,* move on to the next chapter—*animals*!

10

Animals

No one can argue about the way you were a cloud. It was *your* cloud. The *elements of nature* presented you with no problems as to the shape of your body because nature's forces are in no way analogous to human structure. Matters are more complicated when you are working on an animal.

An animal is of a specific size, usually with many human characteristics. For instance, the physical similarities between land mammals and humans—one head with two eyes, two ears, a nose and a mouth, four limbs—may be a trap. The closer the physical structure of the animal is to your own, the more difficult it is for you to merge with the animal's inner life and the easier for you to depict the creature with superficial imitation.

Questions may start flooding your consciousness. Do your arms look like a giraffe's front legs? Or like a bird's wings? Are your legs the shape of a horse's? But it is not the external shape you are pursuing. Your concern is not with form but with feeling.

The animal workshops are the second step toward transforming yourself as an actor into a character. The study of animals enables you to act and react in new ways. Through your Exploration of different animals you will enrich and expand your physical and emotional world.

In order to enhance yourself as an actor with new insights and behavior, you must constantly remind yourself that you are the animal, living the animal's life.

Working on the chosen animal as you worked on your element of nature, you are concerned with absorbing its spirit and becoming one with it. Your goal is to capture and experience the inner life and rhythms of whatever animal you choose to become. Once you absorb this inner life, the substance of its structure, shape, and behavior develop naturally.

In order to "feel" the animal's inner life, your body must be able to respond physically like the animal's. This demands a high degree of training. Therefore, the Tuning Up ignition exercises are particularly important for this section. They should help you to overcome your physical problems through mastery of the requisite physical techniques. A well-disciplined body will adjust almost automatically to the circumstances in which it is placed.

You never know what you will be doing next as an animal. Your actions and reactions are never premeditated. Unlike the preceding or subsequent chapters in Looking Out, your animal Explorations require a partner or a teacher—someone who provides stimulation to your animal character. It is important that unforeseen, actual distractions intrude on your consciousness during this exercise.

In my workshops, I place obstacles in my students' path—a chair, a mop, and so forth. I might toss a pillow at my student actors, cover them with a sheet, spray them with water, touch their fingers or toes, flick the lights off and on, or create a breeze with a fan. Anything to alter the environment during the Explorations. I'll do all that unexpectedly, so that their routine is disrupted. This helps them discover the instinctive responses and the feelings of the creature they are exploring.

If you're working in a group with fellow actors, take turns being the one who will provide this stimulation for your colleagues. Remember that when you're exploring your animal you should never know or anticipate what your partner or teacher or designated group leader will do. As an animal, you must always remain true to your inner self, with responses that are always instinctive, never structured.

The possible number of animal Explorations is virtually infinite. The many species have characteristics that can differ widely from each other. Unlike an element of nature which does not have an emotional life, an animal's feelings will change, depending on the situation. In order to tap some of the hoard of riches that Exploration of the animal contains, the animal workshops should be extensive—each actor should try at least one or two different animals from the five groups or classes of animals I include in this chapter. If possible, spend at least ten sessions on the animal workshops.

To learn from the animal, consider it in its natural environment, not a man-made habitat in which it has been conditioned to artificial responses. This is especially so with animals not meant to be pets. Place a fish in a pond instead of a bowl, a mouse in its hole instead of a cage, a bird in the sky or a tree instead of a cage or an aviary.

The animal Exploration enriches you by the different kinds of life you experience. You do not necessarily have always to be able to define the characteristics clearly, for the experience will remain with you.

The structure of the animal model sessions closely resembles that used for elements of nature. As always, each session begins with a half-hour or so of Tuning Up exercises. While the centering and release exercises are the same as before, the ignition are new. Directly after the ignition exercises you lie in the A position and begin your Exploration of an animal. After twenty to thirty minutes you stop and prepare a short, two- to three-minute Contribution exactly as in the previous chapter's sessions. It's important for actors to see other actors work; through observation your characterization becomes richer and deeper.

The Discussion/Deduction stage is much simpler in the animal workshops than it was before. After approximately fifteen minutes of presentations you should write down a description of your own experience as your particular creature. The writing should flow out spontaneously—don't worry about creating a carefully crafted Pulitzer Prize-winning report.

After you've all written a paragraph or so, each actor should briefly discuss out loud what he or she experienced. Then, going back to their own piece of paper, group members should underline those words or phrases that describe their particular animal's characteristics. These are the "clue words" or "clue phrases" with which a character may be outlined.

The final step is exactly the same as before—Physicalization of a Character. The instrument of this final step is the imaginary situation that each actor should physicalize as fully as possible. Again, you should try two situations—an ideal one and one that is contrary to the nature of your character.

What follows are five model sessions—one each for water creatures, reptiles, insects, birds, and mammals. The first session is written out in the most detail. By now you should have a good sense of how these Looking Out sessions are structured. I have included lots of student examples because as with any acting process you learn a lot through the observation of others.

As I stated before, do more than one of each animal class, if possible. If one type of animal seems to stir the creative juices more than another, spend more time with it. When you're ready to select an animal from a category, always choose the first creature you think of in that classification. Often I'll ask a class to do the same water creature first before I let them choose their own. It may be instructive for your group to do so also—you'll see how differently a seal, a snake, or a hummingbird may be portrayed, even while each characterization exhibits a common ground.

Try not to be concerned with your body in these sessions. Your physical ability is that of the animal on which you are working. The spirit of the animal and its impulses, now yours, create a harmony between the animal's impulses and your actions.

ANIMALS: FIRST MODEL SESSION—WATER CREATURES

Tuning Up

Complete the centering and release exercises for the breath, voice, and body as described on pp. 201–12 in Appendix 1. They are the same as those you did in the previous chapter. The voice and body ignition exercises, however, are different. You'll notice that the body ignitions are more extensive for the animal Explorations than for either the elements of nature or man-made object Explorations. Spend twenty to thirty minutes on the Tuning Up exercises.

Exploration

Begin by lying on your back in the A position, your legs and arms spread out from your body at about forty-five degree angles, palms facing up. Relax, as if in profound sleep. Pay no attention to anyone else. You are going to go deep into a world growing out of your imagination. You are going to become a member of a different species, very different from you in physical structure—a water creature—any animal whose life is dependent on a water environment for survival. Choose the first animal that occurs to you.

Let the process happen as unselfconsciously as possible. Use your imagination to evoke your habitat. Don't move unless the impulse to action stems from your animal being or your animal being responds to an outside influence supplied by a partner or teacher. However, anything may trigger your reactions—sounds, movements, whatever. Try to avoid "gymnastics" or "acrobatics." You have plenty of time in which to undergo this transformation into the new life form you've chosen.

Use the next twenty minutes to become your specific water creature and explore it. Allow yourself to be led by your impulse as the animal, wherever it takes you physically and vocally. Go ahead. You're on your own. Just do it.

Contribution

Now you have ten minutes in which to structure your Contribution, exactly as you did after exploring the different elements of nature. Don't spend more than fifteen minutes on the presentation of the Contributions. Even with a large group of actors, you will all eventually get a chance to share your work in one of these animal sessions.

Discussion/Deduction

Here the Deduction—the analysis—is done a bit differently from that of the elements of nature. Take a pad and pencil and write a paragraph, or even several, describing your experience as the creature you became. Then everyone should take turns reading what they've written. Remember, as I said before, don't worry about the quality of the writing. Just jot down whatever feelings or descriptions that come easily to mind.

After the actors read the description of their own experience aloud, point out the important words and phrases for each of your animal characters. In your group, you should discuss what each actor has written in terms of finding the clue words necessary to point the performer toward a full, rich characterization. Pay special attention to distinctive verbs, adjectives, and adverbs. Disregard selfconscious statements, judgmental phrases, or observations of others. To demonstrate what I mean, here's what Amy came up with for this exercise, with the clue words already underlined:

> I was an octopus. It felt good to swim through the water by bringing my tentacles together. I wanted to attach myself to everything. I was conscious of my suction cups on the undersides of my tentacles. I tried to hold on to rocks, but it was hard. I squirted ink when another animal got too close. I felt such power from my center. The feeling of elasticity in my body was good. But I had a strong feeling of aloneness. I was beautiful, yet others saw me as ugly. I had beautiful black and purple and yellow coloring. Plankton was yummy. I'd like to have babies so I wouldn't be alone. I like the freedom of an octopus.

Amy underwent a genuine emotional experience, except for one small part. When she saw herself through others' eyes as ugly, she fell into a trap of being selfconscious and judgmental instead of letting the action flow freely, out of instantaneous expression. When you're onstage, you are concerned with what you have to do, not with what you look like. That is why Amy didn't underline the adjective "ugly" in the above passage—it refers to a judgment she perceived from others.

Bill really put effort into "being" a turtle, and most of the time it worked. He knew how to take an almost helpless situation, that is, one where he had difficulty in moving, and through insight, used a wave to go on with his work. He managed to merge with his subject. His instincts became strong and true and his sense of being in a different world prevailed:

> Just before hearing the instructions, I heard the words describing the A position, in which our palms are to be face-up. The first thing that popped into my head was a turtle. Subconsciously, I think I may have connected the vulnerability of my palms with the helplessness of a turtle on its back. I could have sat there and died, but I opted to get on with the exercise and catch the next wave into the water.
>
> I embarked on my journey. I was swimming—arms and legs extended, and all at once I felt tired. I stopped and sat. I felt the sand at the bottom, swooshed it around and made a place for myself. It was a cozy feeling, very quiet. I felt peaceful and floating, yet rooted. Sensing danger, I hid my head and allowed myself to feel the warmth inside my shell—the strength of it. I felt secure inside. I felt hungry. I felt safe and warm, so I tried to make hunger real for myself. I thought of dishes that I would love to eat, because seaweed didn't turn me on. I knew I had to extend myself to come out to take a chance to get food.

It is hard to remain a turtle for twenty minutes or so without being distracted, without being reminded of your own body. But when Bill thought of his favorite dishes to stimulate hunger he stepped out of being the turtle. When this happens to you as an actor you need to try to recapture the character by going back to the activity before the distraction—in Bill's case, before his recognition of hunger.

When you play a role, there will always be distractions. You must find the means to regain your concentration through focusing on your actions and intentions, without stepping out of character.

Dan, another student, had a wonderful Exploration of a seal. Note the way his description demonstrates the total identification he made with his water animal:

> I flipped over on my stomach and slapped my feet together. I arched my spine and threw my head back. Suddenly there was a loud noise and I was startled to realize it was coming out of *my* throat. It came out of me again—so loud I was almost frightened. This was my rock I was lying on and everyone else had better keep off. I dragged myself wriggling down to the sea and slid into a wave. It was cool and smooth. I spun around and around in the water and then rolled over and over. I had tremendous feeling of freedom, of control, I dived deep after a fish. I caught and swallowed it in one gulp. Delicious! I lay on my back on the surface, rocked by the sea. I was safe, invulnerable. Suddenly I wanted to scratch my back. I sprang straight up onto the shore. I went to my rock and rubbed my back against it. I roared—almost involuntarily—and then I basked in the sun.

There are several clues in Dan's description to the quality of his exercise. The fact that he said he was "startled" to find noise coming from his throat meant that he had total identification with his seal character and had achieved a strong inner transformation. Everything that happened showed us how personal this exercise was—his attachment to what he called "my" rock is evidence of this transformation. (It is underlined not as a clue word, but to point out the depth of his identification.) The way he behaved as a seal in his environment gave us the feeling that he was completely at home.

Physicalization of a Character

In this workshop, as in others dealing with unspecified animals, you each create your individual situations, based on your own personal Exploration and the resulting clue words that you've gleaned from your Deduction. In each of these model sessions, however, I'll give examples of ideal and conflicting situations for each student whose work I discuss. Study your clue words and phrases, and using my situations here as a guide, come up with scenarios on your own that best fit your specific water creature character's traits.

For Amy, who had explored being an octopus and had come up with clue words like "aloneness" and "holding on," I suggested a situation that would highlight these qualities. I told her she was an orphan who was living in the house in which she had been raised, the house in which her parents and grandparents had lived. She was surrounded by the same furniture and other objects since she was born. She had grown deeply attached to everything and loved it all, feeling herself a part of each of these things. She even knew the kind of light and shadow that played in each room at the different times of day. She loved the smell of the house. The only problem was that now and then an intruder, such as a plumber, a meter reader, or the gardener would enter the house.

For Amy's opposite situation, I suggested that she lived in the same house as before, under the same circumstances, only now she was married. One day she came home to find that without consulting her, her husband had changed the furniture to more modern pieces and had broken through several walls to "improve" the rooms. A large part of the garden was now being occupied by the beginning frame of a new garage. I told her not to only take in the damage, but to imagine what else he had done.

For Bill's situations, the first thing that came to my mind from his turtle character were circumstances that had been in the news a lot at the time—I proposed that he be a farmer for his ideal situation. Everything about his land should be familiar and peaceful. He should go about his daily routine, which had been unchanged for as many years as he could remember. Using his turtle characterization developed from his Exploration and Contribution, Bill imagined a set of circumstances based on this ideal scenario and acted it out.

After five or ten minutes I stopped him and suggested he test his turtle character by imagining this same farmer in an economic crisis that is threatening his property. I told him to imagine a car in the distance full of bankers coming to discuss the foreclosure of his property. He was to complete the same chores, only this time watching the car drawing nearer and nearer.

Dan's seal character was most notable for its sunny disposition. I offered an ideal situation for his characterization: one in which he was the life of a party. He was the center of attention. Everyone sought out his company—to talk or dance with him. He joked with everyone. He was happy and made everybody else happy. Dan then enacted this situation totally, dancing, changing partners, even managing to snatch goodies from the tables as he went.

For Dan's situation in conflict I proposed that he imagine himself at a black tie, high society party at which he knew no one. He was ignored by everybody. The affair was governed by formality and strict protocol, with endlessly dull speeches. He sat at a large table waiting for food while ravaged by hunger. When the speeches were finally over, the food arrived on trays. The portions were despairingly small.

Obviously there is an endless supply of alternatives to these situations. Use your natural creativity to come up with situations of your own that excite your imagination and lead you into an activity that makes full use of everything you've experienced in your Exploration.

ANIMALS:
SECOND MODEL SESSION—REPTILES

Tuning Up

Begin this session as always—by warming up your physical instrument through the exercises you'll find in the Appendix. Those pages should be getting a bit worn by now. Spend the half-hour or so as needed on your centering, release, and ignition exercises.

Exploration

Now lie on the floor in the A position. Relax your body and mind before choosing a reptile that you will become. You don't have to know the creature's specific habits, diet, activities, or even its proper name. Visualize your reptile and then let its essence inhabit your inner being. Let its being and energy merge into yours until it takes over. Maintain your concentration and focus, exploring your animal for at least twenty minutes.

Contribution

In the same way as in previous sessions, take ten minutes to structure a brief presentation for your fellow group members. If your group is large, make sure everyone gets a chance to contribute before someone goes again.

Discussion/Deduction

Now is the time to get out your pad and pencil and write down your experience as a reptile. Write from the gut, without adornment. As you listen to your fellow group members' descriptions, and the subsequent discussion, you should become more aware of how your characterization is unique.

After you've finished your paragraph or two, go back through it and underline those clue words that can be used to create your specific reptile character. Carol, a former student of mine, started out as a lizard. This is her Deduction:

> When I opened my eyes, my first realization was that I existed. I became totally aware of my limbs. My limbs were part of the ground, almost attached to it. Then I became aware of what I was—a lizard. I was a giant lizard, belly and limbs entrapped by the ground, crawling, dragging my powerful frame. My body, heavy and hard, was burdensome to my struggling arms. My movement was slow, and as I searched for food, I longed for a smaller burden. My search became desperate as hunger racked my trunk. Even upon finding food my awareness of my limbs saddened me. I was strong, and because of this I was to know I was no ordinary lizard. I was an alligator.

Carol had a strong emotional identification with her animal. But being aware of a burdensome body and longing for a smaller burden is a selfconscious concept. Any creature accepts its physical structure without question. The concept came from Carol's mind, from her perception. This selfconsciousness could be rooted in a reluctance to allow her own personality to become submerged in that of the alligator, and to let her emotional identification with the alligator to take over completely.

In a role you must abandon resistance to letting the character take over. *Being* the character means you accept yourself without intellectualizing. No matter how noble or evil your actions, you shouldn't think of yourself as a good or a bad person. You are who and what you are.

Frank's description of his Exploration is evidence of how the feelings you bring from the outside into the workshop, and your personal state of being at the outset of the exercises, lead you into executing the exercise and actually choosing the type of animal and its actions:

> I lay on the floor. I could not think, let alone be creative. I didn't want to move. I had had a bad experience at home that made me vulnerable. An incredible fear suddenly overwhelmed me. I was absolutely <u>paralyzed</u>. My body was stiff and hurting. I didn't dare move a finger or an eye. Someone touched my waist. I <u>darted</u> like a bullet, found a space between some bodies, and froze. I <u>didn't</u> want to be touched. I didn't want to be seen. <u>I wanted to disappear</u>.
>
> Then I realized I was a chameleon. As the thought of being a chameleon entered my head, I became even more <u>vulnerable</u>, completely <u>paranoid</u>. My heart was pounding. I was breathing fast and with difficulty. I couldn't control myself. I found myself <u>crawling</u>, <u>hopping</u> all over the place, laughing hysterically. I froze in a corner of the room. I cried quietly, hoping no one was paying attention. I felt relieved. I was thirsty. I crawled to the water fountain in the lobby. I licked the water from the fountain top. I discovered the floor's corners and crawled slowly along. It was easy. I was <u>very light</u>. I was breathing more easily now. My energy was coming back. Someone came close to me. I froze. I faced him in these <u>staccato</u> movements. I was <u>alert</u> but not afraid.

Since Frank's personal feelings and actions were identical to those of the chameleon, I told him to use the clue words from the entire experience, including those phrases underlined above that described the feelings he had before he knew he was a chameleon. Frank's Deduction above is a great example of how an actor's personal life and background contribute to a unique characterization. You will notice that negative statements usually don't yield clue words that are helpful—"I didn't want to move" doesn't guide you to characterization as much as the positive statement "I was absolutely paralyzed."

Physicalization of a Character

Now it's time to test your characterization in some human situations. Using the clue words and phrases that you gleaned from your Deduction, create an ideal situation and enact it fully before switching to the opposite, or conflicting situation.

Carol's alligator suggested a specific physicality to me so I proposed that she imagine herself to be extremely overweight and the maid of honor at her best friend's wedding. I told her that she had important functions at the reception, introducing people, toasting the couple, telling the band when to start playing. Of course, there was food all over the place, in delicious, bountiful supplies.

After she enacted that situation, as a contrast, I told Carol that now she had to lose all her extra weight. She had to go on a strict regimen of minuscule portions at mealtime. Further, every day she'd had to go through a rigorous and strenuous set of exercises to get in shape.

To fulfill the neurotic, crazy energy of Frank's chameleon character I suggested he be an artist dining alone at a fashionable restaurant where many other well-known artists eat. Suddenly he was joined by a magazine interviewer and a photographer who had come to write a story on him. A tape recorder was placed in front of him and flashbulbs went off. All the other artists stared.

Then to stretch his characterization, I told Frank that he was back in his studio, working for an upcoming exhibition. Supremely confident of his work, he tried to concentrate on what he was doing. Did he get a drink? Did he turn the radio on or off? Or did he take the phone off the hook? Frank's response to the absence of pressure to which he could react created its own conflict.

ANIMALS:
THIRD MODEL SESSION—INSECTS

Tuning Up

Begin with your centering, release, and ignition exercises. Do them all! Don't skimp on the basics. Spend about twenty-five minutes Tuning Up.

Exploration

Immediately after you've finished the ignition lie down on your back in the A position. Let all the tension in your thoughts and in your body ooze away.

Choose the first insect or bug that comes to mind and gradually let its being fill your insides. Don't move until the insect's essence drives you to movement. Take your time and let the process happen naturally. Perhaps you won't move or react until the group leader or teacher stimulates your senses in some way. Most importantly, don't force anything.

Contribution

Spend ten minutes directly after your Exploration condensing your experience into a two- to three-minute presentation. Try not to only capture the essence of your specific insect creature, but attempt to include its full range of behavior.

Be an active spectator and audience member for your fellow group members. Be observant as to how a fellow actor's Contribution can "contribute" to your character and experience.

Discussion/Deduction

After the quarter hour or so of Contributions, get out your pad and pencil, and, thinking back to your Exploration, quickly describe how you felt, what you did, what moved you, angered you, tickled you. Then take turns reading aloud what you've just written down. Listen carefully to each other. Try to help spot phrases and clue words for each other, as well as phrases that indicate that an actor hasn't made a full identification.

One student of mine, Dan, had had an unusually bad day. His lack of transformation is evident in the second sentence of his Deduction, where he refers to a specific place he once knew.

> It was very easy for me to become a bug. My impulses directly led me to a pond in Brice Creek, Oregon, where I became a little water bug skimming around, minding my own business. I had fun at first, just bopping around, letting the warm sun make me slow and relaxed. I particularly enjoyed eating microscopic food. After a while, however, I found my life as an insect repetitive and unrewarding. Only eating and swimming led to a dull life.

The point of the Exploration was to identify with the insect that Dan chose to become. But Dan seemed to be having difficulty in letting go of his own memories of Brice Creek so that it never became merely a natural environment for his water bug. When he was bopping around the pond, he *was* the water bug. He actually *felt* the sun, he *relished* his food. But would his bug have cared what was the name of the pond? Was the bopping around having fun an end in itself or was he hunting food or evading enemies?

How dull would eating and swimming be to a creature whose life depended on such activities? Being "dull" is a judgmental observation. As we don't become judgmental of the character we portray onstage, we try not to become judgmental about our subject.

Sometimes actors get caught up in their own personal observations of the Exploration rather than describing their feelings and sensations from the animal's perspective. Usually, this results in a Deduction which doesn't sufficiently build a base for characterization. Take Frank's Deduction as an example:

> As I lay in the A position, the first thing that came into my mind was a visual image of an insect and my feelings when looking at insects. But this became too external. I realized this was nothing like my original human's eye view. Everything, from my mechanics to my ratio of traveling through space, was altered drastically. Knowing that some mammoth human figure was watching my every move, I realized that the human's idea of fast-moving was very slow for me, and that his ideas of sharp movements were clumsy to me. I didn't think about the gigantic/everyday-size objects I crawled over. This was my space, my surroundings. It always had been and always would be.
>
> The feeling of never having been a mammal and being without fur and flesh, or even a reptile's skin, having only an outer shell, was a difficult but reachable challenge. The exercise was eye-opening. To become a different living creature strongly reinforced my belief that dedicated concentration will make everything and anything happen.

It's obvious that Frank's description here doesn't reveal the character from the inside. He must be more specific and less general about what he experienced. Although his imagery has reached our intellect, as actors we need to build an emotional link to what he said. We want to connect with what he felt rather than what he realized.

What did he do when his perception of speed changed? How did he "zoom through space"? Did he fly? Did he scuttle on his little legs? When he became aware of the "giant human," how did he feel? Was he frightened? Was he secure about his superior speed in case he needed to escape? Frank mentioned that this was an "eye-opening" experience for him, so he evidently got a great deal out of it. However, his Deduction gives us nothing on which to build a character. The only possible clue words are "speed" and "crawl." These aren't enough to work with. I suggested that perhaps he should explore the same insect. again, trying to get more into the depth of the insect's life before he try to base a character on it.

Frank then described his experience differently. Here, his earlier intellectualization did not come into play. This new Deduction said what he did and how he felt, and provided a better grip on his character:

> I felt a great sense of freedom. Space did not exist, just changing goals and direction. There was no problem of reaching a goal, all I had to do was hop and there I was. Now here, now there. I was secure in my environment. I was weightless, I had no muscle, just will. I willed to zoom—I zoomed. I willed to stop—I stopped. I felt confident. I was fearless, not afraid of anything. Nothing could get me.

Now through this description, Frank found a way to reach his character physically. Another student, Bill, became a cockroach. Though his Deduction begins like Frank's—with an intellectualization—it quickly becomes clear that his Exploration and subsequent description was one that had a much greater degree of identification than either Dan's or Frank's:

> The roach which I created has nothing which can be called "emotion." Emotion presupposes soul. The roach is soulless. My roach lacks desire, having only drives, instincts—basic instincts which are vital to the survival of a species: eating, reproducing, running away.
>
> Can I stop myself from doing a mating dance? No. The instinct to dance comes from deep inside my abdomen. Can we not control our basic drives? Those which possess us to spring up from the linoleum and arch our bodies into contortions of helpless ecstasy, pain, and rage? My essence is reflex and instinct. I must avoid discomfort. I have no eyelids, so I must hide in a dark place so that the light may not hurt my eyes. I seek water when thirsty. When I die, my final convulsive death throes release my fertile egg sac and liberate my posterity— tens of thousands of new roaches. I am the perfect reproducer.

Of course, a roach knows nothing of souls, including whether or not it has one. Bill chose to become a purely instinctual creature, and as such wouldn't give us factual or metaphysical reasons for its being. However, Bill experienced dancing, contortions, drives, reflexes, ecstasy, pain, rage. All these feelings and the way they were developed physically will supply his store of experience. When he's actively searching for characterization this knowledge will be there for him to draw from.

From this kind of "becoming" you learn that even a little insect, so small as to be almost invisible, has its own life, its own spirit, its own rhythms. A dramatic character based on an insect's physicalization will have its own unique traits, with expressive shadings that are hard to come by otherwise.

Physicalization of a Character

Now comes the time to test out the range and subtlety of your insect characterizations. Drawing upon your clue words and phrases, imagine a situation that would be ideal for your insect. Explore the circumstances fully, enacting the scenario in as specific a manner as possible. Then expand your character by creating a conflicting situation.

For Dan's water bug I thought up this ideal situation: He's a Con Ed meter reader on vacation. He's joined his friends at a health spa because there's nothing better to do. I then suggested that he investigate the sauna, the weightlifting machine, the bikes, the whirlpool, the massage tables, and so on.

To put a spin on this paradise, I propose that he now imagine he's been transferred from reading meters, where he felt comfortable and secure, to a job as an accounting intern. The work is confining and the detail oppressive. He has been trained and is now faced with an enormous stack of work that must be completed by the end of the day.

Frank's clue words—"zoomed," "confident," and "secure" suggested that his character's ideal situation might be something like that of a circus manager who has just come into a new town and must set up the show. The rigging must be hung properly, the performers readied, ticket booth manned, and so on.

Then to complicate this scenario and enhance Frank's insect characterization, I asked him to imagine that the stage hands have suddenly gone on strike. The performers won't leave their dressing rooms, and a growing crowd is becoming impatient outside.

The ideal situation for Bill's "soulless" roach might be as a gangster in a hide-out. All he does is watch the news broadcasts that detail his heinous activities. But he's confident he's safe where he is. He has a good supply of food and everything else he needs. Conveniently, the TV and the radio keep him informed as to what his pursuers are up to.

The reverse situation for such a character might be something like one in which he's been caught and is standing trial. He's dragged into court, exposed to the cameras and questioning of the press, as well as the comments of the crowd. He must stand revealed to the jury and spectators in the courtroom. Afterwards, he must be subjected to the same onslaught of lights and questions as he's brought away from the court, back to jail.

ANIMALS:
FOURTH MODEL SESSION—BIRDS

Tuning Up

Get that instrument in shape! Spend a good half-hour getting your breath, voice, and body warmed up for the Exploration ahead. Begin your Exploration immediately after the ignition exercises.

Exploration

Find a space in the room to lie on your back in the A position. This Exploration will be of birds—choose the first one that comes to your mind. Take the time to make a total identification with the bird. Get inside the bird, let it become you.

When the bird demands vocal or body movement, let yourself go, following your bird's impulses. After at least twenty minutes of exploring your subject, move on to the Contribution.

Contribution

As before, take ten minutes or so to structure and distill your Exploration experience. Take turns sharing your Contributions.

Discussion/Deduction

Now it's time to sit down and write out your description of the experience. Remember that your perceptions are non-judgmental. Describe those feelings and sensations that can be best described in a positive way.

Sometimes students will come up with a Deduction that isn't fully realized. Emily transformed herself into a duck.

My legs shortened and bent backwards at the knees. My arms attached differently in the shoulder sockets and became wings. My feet flattened and webbed between the toes, and the floor turned to mud and water. My center of gravity dropped and when I walked on land my weight was awkward. In the water and, to a lesser extent, in the air, the whole body was more comfortable and familiar.

After she read her description I asked if that was all she had written? "What do you mean?" she wondered. I explained that she had given us a wonderful picture of how totally involved she was in transforming herself into the physical structure of a duck which is very good, but what about the duck's life? Did anything happen?

Emily couldn't think of anything, "I'm afraid there wasn't much more. I used the Exploration time working on the duck's physical structure. I enjoyed experimenting with it."

I told her that what she did was fine. She probably needed the assurance that she could transform physically. It's not unusual to want to be assured that we are capable of it. But now, I told her, "Go back to your duck. Explore it again, living within its environment. Use the physicalization you discovered. Try not to think of it. Allow your surroundings to affect you. You mentioned water. How does it feel when it touches your body? Are you hungry? The food—do you find it in the pond or on land? Are there any distractions? Obstacles? Dangers? Pleasures?"

Emily went and explored being a duck again. She came up with a new Deduction. Notice how her previous concentration on the physical life of the duck resulted in very specific movements she will be able to use in a characterization later:

I assumed the physicality of the duck, and I started by imagining my environment. This wasn't hard. I wanted to plunge into the pond very badly. I had quite a way to walk before getting to it. The limits of my body restricted me. I released a shriek. It was amazing. It freed me to get up from squatting, which was painful. Still shrieking, but now joyously, I ran toward the water. I hopped, my wings fluttering, my weight shifting with each step now to the right now to the left. My neck moved uncontrollably in all directions. I saw something like a bird on the grass in front of me. I stopped at once and stood as still as a statue. But I couldn't control my eyelids. They opened and closed all on their own. My neck followed suit. I was <u>very alert</u>. I drew closer to the bird in <u>jerky movements</u>, stopping after each step. I jumped on the bird, <u>poking</u> it with <u>powerful and fast pecking of my beak</u>. I <u>tore</u> it to pieces <u>viciously</u>. I was crazed. I realized that my shrieks were driving me crazy. I stopped. I didn't want to go on exploring.

Obviously, Emily's second Exploration resulted in a richer, and more specific Deduction. This will become very useful when she works on the Physicalization of a Character through differing situations.

Dan chose an eagle for the subject of his Exploration. He came up with a short and succinct Deduction:

I felt as though I were <u>floating on air</u> as I flew. I felt very <u>centered</u>, very <u>powerful</u>. I saw many <u>things</u>, details from my location that I had not recalled in years. It didn't matter what physical position I took—as an eagle I found that even lying on my back gave me a sensation of flying. Experiencing the <u>height</u>, <u>speed</u>, <u>wind</u> and <u>temperature</u> on my back, I was able to maintain this feeling on my stomach, on my feet, and standing up. I was also able to relate and interact with the other birds.

Dan speaks of deeply felt sensations. His experiences were direct and the identification with the subject of his Exploration was fulfilling and inspired. Now its time to test out your characterization of a bird.

Physicalization of a Character

Using your clue words and phrases as a guide, devise a scenario that your bird character would find ideal. Enact the situation as fully as you can, carrying over as much of the physicality of your bird as possible.

The physical life suggested to me by Emily's duck Deduction was one of a dance choreographer rehearsing her company for an upcoming major recital. The piece is new and the dancers are very supportive and enamored of working with her.

After exploring your ideal situation, it's time to try a conflicting scenario. To put Emily's character in conflict I told her to imagine sitting in the audience at the opening night performance of her new dance piece. She was surrounded by dignitaries from the arts, high-powered politicians, and all her family and best friends. She must sit there as her dancers inexplicably start screwing up everything.

As for Dan's eagle, I suggested a similar situation in which he is a dancer performing a solo before hundreds of people. He's totally immersed in his performance and in full control of the stage and the audience. Then I asked him to try the same situation again only this time in the midst of his performance, the orchestra suddenly plays the wrong music. He must continue, nevertheless.

ANIMALS:
FIFTH MODEL SESSION—MAMMALS

Tuning Up

Start with your centering, release, and ignition exercises. By now you shouldn't even have to turn to pp. 201–17, except to remind yourself that you haven't forgotten any part of the Tuning Up process.

Exploration

Lie comfortably on your back in the A position and relax your mind and body. Choose a mammal, and without forcing the identification, slip into its skin and let its nerves, bones, and sinews become yours. Take your time to let the transformation occur completely.

Then let your animal's energy move you. Allow your Exploration to go on for twenty or even thirty minutes. By now your concentration and focus should be highly developed.

Contribution

Condense your Exploration experiences into a short, structured piece to present to your fellow group members.

Discussion/Deduction

Hopefully by now you are becoming expert at describing your animal Explorations and making helpful Deductions. From experience, however, I know only too well that it is easy to fall into old habits. Although Bill made certain inroads into being a cat, he started with an observation rather than emptying himself so that he could be filled with the spirit of his subject:

> Back home I have a cat I love dearly. For years I had watched her every move, the grace and the indifference she would often radiate. In my

transformation into being a cat, I was aware of human beings playing with me when I didn't feel like it. I had to outguess their sudden impulses to cruelty or ignore them for the time being. Graceful, powerful, I felt no need to use the cat's vocal chords until the hunger pains grew intense and I begged for human help of some kind.

As you can see, the above clue words don't yield a very complex insight into a character. The way Bill talks of "the cat's vocal cords" instead of writing in the first person is another indication that his transformation into a cat wasn't very complete. He never stopped resorting to planned actions, situations, and memory.

Dan was much more successful becoming a dog. He furnished the following Deduction:

I was a bassett hound. Short legs, stumpy. Weight very low to the ground. When I'd lie down, the weight toppled me onto my side. The walk was mopey, a comfortable pace for your average, everyday happy hound.

Gail [another student] bit me when I tried to eat her. I yelped but soon I forgot what I was crying about. My attention span, like my rhythms was limited, dulled, and in a word, short-sighted.

I joined the class in congratulating Dan on achieving his life's ambition. He made a fine dog and I'm proud to be in some way responsible. I'm sure Dan learned something from this experience: when you try to eat a fellow actor, you're lucky to escape with your hide intact.

Finally, I'd like to include here a Deduction by Frank. It is noteworthy for its completeness and for the range of emotions which he experienced. If you can squeeze out such a Deduction every time you'll be well on your way to creating detailed, fascinating, and lively characters for the stage. Frank became a lion:

I felt an inner calm. Nothing could be threatening to me—not a thing, nor any creature. I was in absolute authority in any circumstance I found myself in. I felt no special need to use my voice. When I used it, it was to express satisfaction and the sense of well-being. At times I used it to assert authority, but I never felt I had to overdo it. A little bit of voice, a little bit of movement were just enough. Even when I ran it was from an impulse to release inner energy.

Most of the time I felt very wise. It was a wisdom that derived from utter confidence in my being. I sensed sound which I could not comprehend. To begin with, I just felt indignant. Then I became irritated, but after a while I lost interest in the sound. When it was sudden and loud, it struck me almost physically. I sensed it with my entire body. I was furious, and as the sound continued, it drove me out of my wits and out of control. I couldn't resort to any usual action or thing which would help me to regain some control, to find my center. I was out of myself. I felt beaten physically. The sound caused me confusion, lack of center, lack of focus, and it extended for a long time. My nerves were tense. I became hungry. It was a need that rose from the depth of my guts. I became impatient. Good nature and generosity gave way to straight anger. As I was seeking food, my anger erupted. I saw nothing but blood. I was wronged. Food should have been there. I was about to destroy all that was on my way. When I discovered my prey, it was no longer food but an enemy. I tore it to pieces and only with the taste of its blood did I come back to my senses.

As I ate, my good nature crept back into me. I felt loving and generous. I became sleepy and lazy. I was willing to accept any silly thing the other creatures did around me. I was in a mood to be amused. I felt paternal. All creatures became my own children. When things did not amuse me, I was indifferent to them.

Frank's identification with his subject was as complete and deeply felt as one could wish it to be. No matter whether he was serene or angry, confused or positive, he never lost his sense of omnipotence.

Physicalization of a Character

Now is the time to put these characterizations to the test. You should be gathering your clue words and phrases and creating imaginative ideal and conflicting situations. By now you may have noticed that the bigger your list of clue words, the more possibilities you have. That's why it is beneficial to write detailed Deductions.

For Bill's cat character I suggested that he be a high-powered executive who has just been promoted and given a lavishly appointed new office. Enacting this situation, he could luxuriate in his new executive chair and inspect his elegant mahogany desk, take in the resplendent views from the tall glass windows. To make this situation more challenging, I proposed that he walk in to his office to get his papers ready for his first meeting with the president of the company only to find his papers and files scattered all over the place. He tries desperately to get things in order. He hears footsteps, a knock.

A night watchman is what I thought of after reading Dan's basset hound Deduction. His situation would be a comfortable one, where he had little to do but amble around the factory plant and then scoot back to his office to watch TV and nap. A conflicting situation should be obvious—his night watch routine is interrupted by a burglar alarm and he suddenly finds himself in a shoot-out.

Because Frank's lion Deduction was so rich and varied, I told him that he should only work on one aspect of the beast's personality—it is not necessary to deal with the entire spectrum of his emotions. Therefore, I selected the first phase, where his lion was calm, strong, and untroubled. I told him to imagine he is on a battlefield, the commanding general of a triumphant army which is sweeping all before it. He directs operations without a doubt as to the wisdom of his decision.

For a conflicting situation, I proposed that Frank survey the destruction he's inflicted after the battle is over. He is aware of the massive loss of lives that has resulted from his decisions. Then he's confronted by his commanding officer who informs him that he has overstepped his authority and is therefore relieved of his command.

In all these situations, remember that the point is to bring the physical life you have developed through your Exploration of an animal and your subsequent Contribution into a human situation. Don't drop your essential physical and emotional characteristics, even when the circumstances challenge it most.

11

Man-Made Objects

In the *man-made objects* study, for the first time, the actor initiates the stimulus. You call on your imagination in a new way to create what the object's feelings and activities would be if it had an emotional life and if it could act. You physicalize a completely new life, creating a new being, bringing to it all you are capable of.

You could neither create nor dominate the elements of nature, nor could you truly enter animal forms. The stimulus to your creativity came from the elements and the animals and you responded by letting them work on you through your senses and emotions.

The study of *man-made objects* teaches you to create. It is the third and final step toward transforming yourself as an actor into a character.

Most often, we take every-day, functional objects for granted. We use and accept them as naturally as we accept the sun, the rain, or a tree. Yet the tree and the door knob evolved differently. The tree grew, but the door knob was shaped solely by human hands and minds. When you do these Explorations, you may find yourself awestruck as you reexamine a pin, a carpet, or an airplane with fresh eyes.

In the two preceding studies, you opened yourself passively. You were a receptacle absorbing the spirit and lives of the elements and animals.

Now, although you keep yourself open, your creative powers remain active. You should select a specific object to work on—a chair, a broom, a balloon, a clock, a bicycle—deliberately observing the object with your mind's eye. You will study its life as if it were physically present. Your imagination and emotions will infuse life into it and then you will become the object itself.

Unlike the previous two chapters, I will not include a number of model sessions. Instead, I will explain just one session and then you should explore at least three different objects.

Often, as the teacher, I will start by assigning an object for the entire group to portray—a balloon, for instance. This is always useful the first time so that you can understand the purposes and inner workings of the process without worrying about your choice of object.

The man-made object work can be done alone, though it will become obvious that a large group may be utilized in an interesting way when I explain how situations are created. Have fun choosing your object—from it you will truly be "creating" a character.

MAN-MADE OBJECTS: MODEL SESSION

Tuning Up

You'll find these exercises are as important to do fully as they always were. The only change from the previous chapters' work comes in the voice and body ignition. You'll find the exercises on pp. 201–17. Take your time and complete all the exercises, spending about twenty or thirty minutes on them.

Exploration

As in the previous chapters in this section, lie on your back in the A position. This time you're going to work on an object. Close your eyes. Don't force yourself to think of the object. Just relax until your selected object comes to your mind's eye of its own accord. Observe its size, its color, its shape—whatever you need to know about it. Remain relaxed. Try to lose yourself in your object. Immerse yourself in it. Study every detail.

Then watch it begin to breathe, to swell, to stir, to float, to leap, to sleep, to take on its own life and actions. Suppress nothing the object does in your mind. When you are replete with its spirit, become the object and live its life.

In my experience, these man-made object Explorations are wonderful in their creativity. As you'll see from the number of student examples I've included, simple household objects may never look the same to you.

Contribution

This part of the process is exactly the same as with elements of nature and animals. Take ten minutes to condense, distill, and structure a short, two- to three-minute presentation. Then your group should spend about fifteen minutes each session watching several actors present their Contribution.

Discussion/Deduction

As in the previous chapter, take a pencil and a piece of paper and write a paragraph or two describing your experiences as your object. Then go back and underline the clue words and phrases which describe your object's characteristics. As before, focus on the specific feelings and sensations you experienced, more than any thoughts, ideas, or intellectual theories that may have occurred to you during your Exploration.

Amy had decided to explore a clear Lucite candleholder in the shape of a nine-pointed star. Here's her Deduction of the experience:

> I remember the <u>sharp points</u>, the reflections of light coming through the <u>four-sided legs</u>, the hole in the middle to hold the base of the candle. How <u>delicate</u> it looked, yet how <u>strong</u> it really was! <u>Light</u>, <u>lyrical</u>, almost <u>waltz-like tunes</u> began to filter into my ears. I began to hum along. I could feel my legs, arms, and head becoming <u>pointed</u>, <u>dimensional</u>, and <u>glistening</u>. I slowly toppled from point to point with the music and discovered through the awkwardness, the <u>grace</u> with which I moved. I felt as though I were <u>lapping up the melody</u>. I felt <u>happy</u>, <u>playful</u>, <u>serene</u>, and <u>luminescent</u> all at once.

Amy's Deduction makes her Exploration sound like a wonderfully happy experience. She found some clearly defined qualities and, luckily for her, she was inspired and carried away by her imaginary melody into complete inner and physical transformation.

Physicalization of a Character

This process of physicalization isn't the same one you followed in *animals*. In *animals* for each Deduction and set of clue phrases, you acted out an ideal situation and a situation in conflict. The process with *man-made objects* is a little different.

When I'm conducting my workshops, I offer examples of three different characters to each student and let the actors select the one that best fits their personal experience. They then place their chosen character into an imaginary situation. By "character" I don't mean the dramatic creations from a specific play but archetypal, societal roles: a telephone repairman, a mailman, a pickpocket, a beautician. By choosing characters by occupation, situations will naturally suggest themselves.

If you're working in a group, have a partner or group leader read your Deduction and suggest several characters appropriate to your experience. If you're on your own, you should try to enact fully a number of characters that come to mind given your specific clue words. See which situations bring out the physical life of your object best.

Each situation must be complete. Create your own circumstances with your imagination and when you act them make them as real as possible. Because you know what object you are, and where you are, and who your character is, you should allow your actions to evolve naturally.

Don't hesitate to use words if they occur spontaneously to you. However, when you speak you are obviously "thinking." Thinking of words is frequently at the expense of physical expression. Struggle to maintain your physicalization. Any words spoken must surge impulsively, emanating from what is happening to the character in the situation at that very moment.

You may work with a partner. Each of you becomes your character in an imaginary situation that you've both agreed upon. Keep the work flowing. Don't plan out events so much that you begin anticipating what may happen next. You should maintain what I like to call "a spontaneous dialogue of action."

You may even want to let the work evolve into a group situation. For example, based on Amy's Exploration of a candleholder, I proposed three characters: a beauty pageant contestant, an artist receiving an award, or a nun working with poor children. Amy decided to be the beauty queen, and she asked the other actors in the group to portray the contestants, the emcee, the singers, the audience, and the photographers.

If you decide you are a chef planning an important dinner for a great personality, your fellow actors could be kitchen workers, waiters, and so on. If you choose to be a labor negotiator, the other actors might be members of the disputing parties, TV cameramen, newspaper reporters. The only limit is your imagination, which means there is no limit at all.

Remember that once again the purpose of these situations is to reinforce, expand, and apply the characteristic physical life that you discovered through your Exploration of a man-made object. Even when you're surrounded by the chaos and hustle and bustle of a situation enacted by your entire group, hold on to the emotional and physical aspects that transform you into your character.

In fact, don't shy away from physicalizing your character to the extreme. Don't aim for subtleties here. Subtlety will develop later on as you work on characters in a play.

LEARNING BY EXAMPLE

One of the most important aspects of any acting study is watching and observing your fellow actors, either in acting classes, or onstage. Therefore, what follows are a number of sample man-made object Deductions that I've culled from my classes. They all describe a student actor's Exploration with the important clue words and phrases underlined.

This should be particularly useful to those of you who aren't presently working with a group of actors. Let my former students be your group and you'll see how they handled these object exercises. Anyway, you've met most of them already in the previous chapters.

After each Deduction, I make some comments and then suggest a few characters each actor might want to portray in his or her own situation. Feel free to glance through all these character suggestions and use any that would seem to fit your personal Exploration of a man-made object.

Bill focused on a pair of tweezers. Taking his time he carefully observed each aspect of the object and let it come to life, eventually allowing it to take over his being. Here's his Deduction:

I wanted the tweezers to function without outside help, so I envisioned them as searching for prey. As I became the tweezers, my movements were small and very exact and sharp, like a bird's. I felt cold, evil, and pragmatic at times. At others, I felt playful. I had tunnel vision. My eyes focused on very small things and I studied them closely and considered them before I ate them, or picked or plucked them. I was very precise.

This is an excellent summary of Bill's experience. What he has described will provide him with good material to draw upon as an actor. He created a character with a point of view and sharply defined characteristics. These were the characters that suggested themselves to me:

- the President's bodyguard
- a surgeon
- a French chef

Dan decided to explore being a vacuum cleaner. His Exploration and subsequent Deduction were exemplary, as you'll see:

I had a huge, hollow belly and an anguished thirst to fill the void. Except for the belly, every part of my body became a dry, open throat—a sucking tool. My hands, knees, armpits, head, ears, mouth—all were desperately trying to quench the thirst, to fill my belly by sucking in everything that existed. Now it was my arm straining to be filled, now my mouth, now all parts of me together. The dust, papers on the floor, a handbag in the corner, the carpet, the walls.

I was rolling, crawling, climbing, first in one direction, then in others. Nothing could stop me, but my thirst and emptiness were unquenchable, unfillable. My sense of despair was so great I started to cry. It wasn't until after the Exploration was over that I realized how exhausted I was.

This is what an Exploration should be about. Dan really became the vacuum cleaner, really felt what the vacuum cleaner could have felt. It was wonderful how every part of his body became a functioning part of the machine. His description also demonstrates how *physical* this work should be—that is why I call it "a physical approach to acting." I suggested to Dan the following characters from which he might choose:

- a kleptomaniac
- a postal worker
- a factory worker

Frank decided to become a clock. Notice in his description of his Exploration how he went from chaotic activity to controlled, self-contained movement. It was at that stage that he found such fun in his experience that he didn't want to stop:

> I had to move in staccato-like actions. I sat, lay down, got up. I went to bed, but I was restless and frustrated and couldn't sleep. I tossed from side to side, now kneeling, now on my elbows, now on my head. It was a kind of contained chaos. I couldn't find my center. My body split— now the head, the eyes, the arms and legs—each going its own way chaotically with a reason I couldn't comprehend. It struck me funny. I started to sing "Jingle Bells," in staccato, of course.
>
> Then I began to enjoy being a clock. I felt I was gaining control, willing the movement. I was having fun exploring the strange shapes and actions. I kept reenergizing.

Frank's experience shows how completely one can become immersed in the Exploration of a man-made object. It may not happen right away, but when it does the actor is transformed and begins feeding off his or her creation. As Frank told me afterwards, "If you hadn't stopped us, I could've gone on like that forever."

From his insistence on staccato movements and the word "elbows" in his Deduction above, I thought of these three possible characters:

- a traffic cop
- a mailroom sorter
- a theater-usher

Carol had an especially interesting Exploration. On this particular day she had come to class very tired. She confided that when she first started the exercise by lying on the floor in the A position, all she wanted was to sleep. Ironically, her chosen object was a pressure cooker. This is her Deduction:

> I closed my eyes, took a deep breath, and said inwardly, "Goodbye, Moni!" and was half asleep when I was startled by a burst of loud laughter. I became angry instantly. My limbs were numb but I was furious and started cursing. As if in a dream I heard you say, "Make sure to find your way back to the object in spite of distractions." Only then I realized that there was an awful noise of sirens just outside the building. I was furious. "Fuck you, sirens!" I repeated that a hundred times. As

I was saying that, the thought occurred that I was stuck, with no place to go. "I can't hit you, noise," I thought, or do anything about the sirens, which made me even more furious.

A pressure cooker, a pressure cooker. I started shaking all over, yelling, pouting, crying. Finally I heard the laughter again. It was catchy. I started laughing and laughing. But I was trapped, frustrated. My mind was racing. I couldn't go on anymore. I had to calm down.

Like Frank, Carol began slowly, gradually becoming immersed in her object. This is a lesson—don't worry if the transformation doesn't happen right away. Relax, remain open, and it will come. Afterwards, Carol confessed, "I didn't know whether what I went through took a minute or an hour, but I was sure glad to hear your voice again telling me to take a deep breath. It was like waking up from darkness into light."

Again, we see how a personal, emotional state of being transforms and uses its energy creatively. Carol's frustration and entrapment were well felt and described. It makes us aware of the pressure-cooker situation in which we live a great deal of our life, especially here in New York. Everyone can identify with that kind of experience. The kinds of character situations that I thought would be appropriate to Carol's experience were:

- a substitute teacher with a classroom of wild kids
- a hostess in the middle of a screaming fight with her mate when dinner guests arrive
- a playwright attending an opening night of her play and the production is awful

What follows is a sample list of more characters from which you can choose. Try to pick ones that appeal to the characteristic physicality you uncovered in your Exploration:

- defense lawyer
- business executive
- nurse
- police officer
- furniture mover
- gangster

- drug dealer
- pimp
- stage director
- movie director
- secretary
- an extra in a film
- bank teller
- fashion model
- fashion photographer

LOOKING BACK AT
LOOKING OUT: A SUMMARY

The study of the three classifications of subjects developed theatrical, physical, instinctual responses to given situations, without having used memories from your personal lives. Instead you used your imagination and the three subjects of Exploration.

The *elements of nature* taught you to be—to exist.

The *animals* taught you to act and react.

The *man-made objects* taught you to create.

The mere fact that there is a physical presence does not mean there is a physicalized character. Anyone can put on a costume and make-up, memorize lines, and enter and exit on cue. Being able to transform yourself into the character is what makes you an actor.

Characterization means specificity. The character's choices of action are never general, but always specific.

To recap, the steps toward transformation are:

Tuning Up.   These exercises ready the actor physically while clearing the mind of distractions. The exercises evolve from what is natural to the body. The three steps in the Tuning Up process are centering, release, and ignition.

Exploration.   This is the heart of the study, a spontaneous, extremely physical, memory-free, non-intellectual process that springs from an actor's innermost creativity, employing the actor's entire instrument.

Contribution.   This step teaches the actor to shape, structure, and refine his or her acting discoveries that were uncovered in the Exploration. This skill will be useful during a rehearsal process by allowing actors to retain and repeat discoveries later in performance.

Discussion/Deduction.   The step that sharpens the actor's understanding of the creative process. It adds insight to the means of overcoming difficulties with concentration and focus, and helps the actor make a very specific analysis, necessary in order to create full characterizations.

Physicalization of a Character.   The final step wherein the actor uses imaginary situations to develop and practice the discoveries made in the Exploration.

Looking Out has been the second major stage toward characterization. Next comes "Creating a Character" where you combine the transformation techniques you acquired in this section with what you discovered about your *selves* in Looking In.

PART III

CREATING A
CHARACTER

12

Approaching a Role

In Looking In you learned to understand aspects of your own emotional structure so as to identify with the same qualities in others. Looking Out gave you the techniques to transform yourself physically into a character for the stage. You are ready to integrate both. You are ready to assume a role, to create a believable human being—to act.

Now for the first time you turn to a written text. In it you'll find a variety of thoughts and emotions contained in all sorts of situations. Your tools—the body and voice—are used not only to support the words and invest them with life, but to enhance and further the author's ideas by portraying the characters with flexibility, power, and texture.

It is always the character that guides you in your actions. Otherwise, movement becomes gesticulation and the voice empty of meaning. Whether you move or are still, everything must spring from your character's inner life. No outer consideration or esthetic should be imposed.

When you assume a role, you must be nonjudgmental. You do not think of doing "good" or doing "evil." You merely do what is natural to your character. In *Death of a Salesman*, Willy Loman, for instance, sees himself as strong and logical, a victim of circumstance. In actuality, he takes refuge from reality in fantasy, in his baseless dreams for the future. In Molière's *The Misanthrope*, Arsinoë is convinced that everyone is taking advantage of her. She backbites her "friends" and cheats her servants before they can do the same to her. She does not consider herself hypocritical or devious but only a poor defenseless woman looking out for herself the best way she can. Willy and Arsinoë live in ways that are natural to their character.

In this last section I use twelve sample roles chosen from a range of classical and contemporary works. There are six male and six female roles—one of each gender for each of the six *selves* we encountered in Looking In. Dramatic literature is rarely so easily structured. Don't be deceived by the simplicity with which I've grouped these characters. It is for workshop purposes only.

Through these twelve examples you should understand how the *selves* are your emotional link to the character and the basis on which to build it, and how the exploration of a variety of subjects gives you the techniques to transform yourself physically, with the subtleties of detail that bring your character convincingly and truthfully to life.

Reading for Clues

The first step in approaching a role is simple—read the play. And read it again. And again. Every time you go through the text, your knowledge of the characters and world of the play will increase. If you want to be a mediocre actor, quickly read the play through once. If you want to create a character of substance and depth, even if you're performing a scene in a class or workshop, spend time with the play.

Be an active reader. Instead of letting the words blur by your eyes so you can get through to the end, or to your character's next bit of dialogue, read carefully. Highlight phrases and words that describe your role in the play. In the margins jot notes of any impressions or events that are important to your character, or that you might find useful later on.

To define the character's qualities best, watch out for clue words or phrases. You will need to keep a list of the clue words that define your part's characteristics. Because you are now working with a text in which the playwright has given you a role, a story, and an environment, you have a ready-made structure to which you must adhere. This list that you make will be your map and guide.

This is exactly opposite from the way you worked in Looking Out, where you sought the clue words after your unfettered imagination had created Explorations. Here, your key words grow out of your objective analysis of the character as you understand the author's intentions, not through your experience of the Exploration. Now you will base your choice of subjects in your Exploration on your key words and phrases—they are the clues to enable you to physicalize your character. Read carefully and create a thoughtful list of words and phrases.

After you've done this but before moving on, write a one-paragraph summary of the script with emphasis on your character's part in it. This is not an analysis. It is a simple, terse recapitulation of the most important facts as they relate to your role. This summation, along with your list of clue words, will guide you to the character's *self*.

Finding the Dominant Self

You know that no person is one-faceted. In even the simplest character, all actors must be aware of nuances and complexities and adopt them into their interpretations when appropriate, as guided by the clue words. For the purpose of this study, however, I suggest selecting the one aspect of the character's *self* that is most dominant.

You worked on that *self* in detail in Looking In. You experienced the way the *selves* feel, so you will understand your character on a gut level, and be able automatically to link up with the role emotionally. Later on you can work on the character's less dominant *selves* as they emerge in particular scenes or situations.

As an actor you will be called on to play a number of characters who are dominated by their *vulnerable selves, decisive selves*, and so on, but it does not follow that all the *selves* in the same classification are played the same way. Playwrights set forth conditions and circumstances in each of their plays, inventing characters that may be very unlike each other. All dramatic characters live in their own time and place, among different persons with whom they act and react. Each comes from a unique family, with varying social and economic structures, and individual patterns of behavior.

If two actors decide to play the same role and decide to incorporate the same dominant *self* into their interpretation, the result will never be identical. When expressing tension for example, one actor may drum his fingers, another may tap his foot, and a third may freeze, immobile. Any of the innumerable possibilities is correct, provided it springs from the truth of the character—that is, being consistent with the character's overall make-up—and is not an artificially contrived mannerism. Because there are so many, many ways meaning may be expressed physically, describing a particular actor's movements can often be limiting and self-defeating to the reader's imagination.

   Once you have a list of clue words, a one-paragraph summary of the play from your character's perspective, and have chosen a dominant *self* for the role, you are ready to start. If it suits you, think of this preceding preparation as your homework—and don't come to class without it.

Tuning

Whenever you're prepared to begin any acting activity you should begin by Tuning Up. Go through the centering, release, and ignition exercises on pp. 201–17 in the Appendix. Try doing the voice ignition with all three subjects—*elements of nature, animals,* and *man-made objects.* It isn't necessary to do all the body ignition exercises from each subject, but don't do less than a total of twenty minutes of Tuning Up.

   There's a second part of Tuning that is crucial for the process of approaching a role—you must repeat a Tuning In exercise from Looking In. Choose any exercise from the chapter on your character's dominant *self.* If you're working on Iago, from Shakespeare's *Othello,* let's say, and after a careful analysis, have decided that he is dominated by his *social self,* then do a "masking the emotions" exercise from Chapter 4. If you're working on Laura from *The Glass Menagerie* and you've determined her to be dominated by her *vulnerable self,* go back to Chapter Two and try working on one of the physical flaw exercises. This will connect you on an emotional, visceral level with the character you'll be working on. Properly attuned, you'll be ready for the Exploration.

Exploration

The same clue words which helped you to find the character's dominant *self* will also influence your choice of subjects for your Exploration. This Exploration is executed in exactly the same way as in

Looking Out—except for one major difference. It is a Combination Exploration, wherein you practice shifting rapidly from one subject to another. You've had some experience already doing this—in the last *elements of nature* model session you explored a number of different subjects.

Here, the first step is choosing your subjects. Select three—one element of nature, one animal, and one man-made object—consciously basing your choice on your character's clue words. The selection will be influenced as well by the way you feel about the dominant *self.*

Your selections should have something in common with each other as well as with the traits of the *self* you select. It is not similarities of outward appearance we are looking for, but similarities in the subjects' rhythms, movements, moods, or feelings. For example, a river, a seal, and a ribbon all indicate similar attributes of openness and ease, and perhaps if your character's clue words included lightness, agility, flexibility, and freedom, you might have chosen those same subjects.

To illustrate, when you think of Iago, you might think of a rat or a weasel or a snake—creatures that survive through cunning and stealth. Medea might make you think of a lioness—proud, fierce, angry enough to disregard the consequences of her actions. It is highly unlikely that you could think of Iago as a lion, or conversely, Medea as a weasel.

When you are ready to explore your subjects get into the A position and physically relax your muscles so you won't be taxed. Start with your element of nature and explore it fully, eventually letting your chosen animal take over. After you have explored the animal and added its essence to that of the element, concentrate on becoming one with your man-made object. Once you've done this, move from object to animal to element and vary the order as one would naturally evolve from another, without planning. The change from one to another may occur even before an action is completed.

The length of time you devote to one subject before you go on to the next is not important. Keep within you the space to let things happen, and they will. Don't try to be as "fair" to one subject as to another. You might want to work on one subject a relatively long time. The subjects should live, fuse, separate, and fuse again naturally, without planning. If they urge you to sound, it should not be suppressed. If they don't insist, don't force sound to come. It is always the impulse that dictates when the transition should happen and the transformation take place.

While exploring your selected element, you may grow to feel that another is more right for you in the given situation. Don't hesitate to switch from being a sandstorm to a whirlpool, for example. The same is the case with being an animal or an object. If it develops that being a shark is truer for you than being a butterfly, be true to your feelings. Or if both are true for you, if the need arises to experience both, do so. There are no rules to box in your creativity.

Not everything you explore will have the same degree of intensity. Not everything will evoke the same focus of energies. Not achieving the highest possible level of physicality doesn't mean you have not been successful in your Exploration.

The Combination Exploration trains you as the actor to move from one emotion, one thought, one situation to another, varying the shadings of the physicalization while keeping the essence of the character. Although the subjects that you physicalize may be similar since they were suggested by the same set of clue words, the rhythms and characteristics of each subject develop different subtleties. Eventually, this will give you a more extensive vocabulary of movement and interpretation to invest in your characterization.

If this process seems confusing, don't worry. In the following chapters it will become increasingly clear as I describe sample Explorations that some of my students have contributed.

Physicalization of a Character

Whereas in past sessions we followed our Explorations by enacting imaginary situations, here we already have our circumstances prepared for us—those which the playwright has invented.

Before working on a scene or monologue from your character's play, try gaining some command of your character's physicality by enacting simple everyday situations—wake up, brush your teeth, take out the trash, prepare breakfast, get dressed—any routine activities appropriate for your character. In this way you will be better able to incorporate your character's physicality into the roles you choose to portray.

Now select a scene or monologue from the play in which your character appears and prepare to present it for the next session. As I've said several times, these characters are analyzed in order to choose the one archetypal, dominant aspect. Therefore, regardless of the other *selves* that may emerge in various scenes, when you select a scene to work on, it must reflect the *self* that is most consistent during the major part of the play. Bring to the scene what you learned from your Exploration and your understanding of the self.

Up to now in this process your goal has been to create a character—to know that character inside out, on a visceral, emotional basis. You have learned how the character physically acts and reacts. Reread the whole play, not just your part, as many times as necessary, to understand the author's concept of the play and your character's contribution to its development. The play sets forth the circumstances in which your character exists. All the choices for your behavior will grow out of who the character is. All the techniques you have developed can be applied here.

Don't hesitate to wear make-up or costumes, or to work with props, if you feel they will help to support your characterization. The work in this section offers much that the individual actor can do alone, without having to be part of a group. When you choose a scene, for example, you may choose a monologue. If, however, you are part of a group, you may have one or more partners participate in your scene.

In case you have difficulty with your characterization, turn back to the Exploration and in rapid succession reexplore the combination of the subjects you chose, alternating between the element and your character, the animal and your character, and the object and your character. If you're working with other actors, do this Exploration in front of them and keep at it until you break through to the essence of the character's physicalization.

If you're still experiencing problems, the reason may be because you have selected a subject with which you cannot identify totally, and therefore it does not help you to penetrate the character. If this is so, change the subject.

You may concentrate on the same play, the same character, even the same scene for as many sessions as you believe necessary to explore the characterization thoroughly, before you take up a new character. In a class we may work on one or more characters. For the sake of clarity in the student examples that follow, each role to be worked on will be dealt with individually.

I want to emphasize here that the twelve student demonstrations I've chosen are just that—demonstrations. It seems to me that this is the best way to describe and communicate the process by which I teach acting. Of course, students never present material in such a structured order—one female, one male, presenting two characters with the same dominant *self.*

Remember, the process is what is most important. You should note how each of the students uses his or her analysis, clue words, summary, and choice of dominant *self* to select three appropriate subjects. The Exploration of these subjects then provides the basis for the interpretation and physicalization of the character.

13

Approaching
Vulnerable Roles

BLANCHE DUBOIS

In one of my classes, an actress wanted to work on Blanche, Tennessee Williams' classic role from his play *A Streetcar Named Desire*. Amy came to class with her homework done—she had read through the play several times, and had written a summary and a list of clue words. I asked her if she had written out the summary from Blanche's point of view, including all events that shaped her character and actions. Amy supplied the following synopsis:

> Blanche DuBois, born into a formerly aristocratic Southern family, lives in her own world, avoiding reality. Only when she was forced to did she recognize that her young husband was a homosexual. Her guilt for his suicide has driven her into the arms of passing strangers, searching for solace. She has no financial or emotional reserves. She moves in with her sister Stella, who is married to Stanley, a primal, animalistic blue-collar worker. He mocks Blanche's sensitivity and need for beauty and sees through her fantasy defenses. He destroys the relationship between one of his friends and Blanche which could have led to marriage. While Stella is in the hospital bearing his child,

Blanche is raped by Stanley and is driven more deeply into her dream world and a mental institution.

Notice how Amy's summary pretty well captures the play's narrative from Blanche's perspective. Obviously, if Stanley were to summarize the play, the description of events, the adjectives used, and the point of view would all be very different. Amy may have skipped over Blanche's brief romantic attachment to Mitch a little too blithely—it is an important part of her character's arc. Nevertheless, her use of such phrases as "searching for solace," "emotional reserves," and her description of Stanley as a "primal, animalistic" worker are very much choices Blanche herself might make.

I asked her, as I do all my students, to read the summary first so that the rest of her fellow actors would understand what they are about to see, if they themselves hadn't read the play. Amy then read her list of clue words that she had gleaned from her careful readings:

Frail, vulnerable, fragile, unstable, on the verge, taut, terrified, panic stricken, befogged, esthetic, vague, poetic, semi-conscious, needful, fantasizing, dependent, unrealistic, guilty, soiled, wounded, broken, passive, desperate, seductive, graceful, charming, manipulative, feminine, sensuous, lost.

Her next task was to choose a dominant *self* for Blanche. In my workshops, this is always done in the form of a discussion. As you'll see, often actors will have differing interpretations of a character's dominant *self*. Amy informed us that she had decided that Blanche was predominately a vulnerable character.

I asked if she had any questions or problems coming to that decision, but Amy was adamant, "I thought Blanche was singularly clear as to what her dominant *self* was—there wasn't one scene in which I wasn't aware of her vulnerability." And in this case, Amy seemed to be right. You could be mistaken into making a case for Blanche being dominated by her *social self* because of the way she masks reality, but she doesn't realize she's being deceitful, or living in a fantasy world. Any masking she's doing is subconscious. Blanche, in fact, may be the archetypal *vulnerable self*.

Amy's next task was to Tune Up and then work briefly on a *vulnerable self* exercise, choosing a physical flaw, visualizing it fully, and then physicalizing it. This step serves to reconnect her to her own personal vulnerability, thereby forming the emotional basis of her characterization.

In my workshops I then move on to another student as Amy does her centering, release, and ignition exercises. Amy completes her Looking In exercise and comes back to me when she is finished. I then asked her to choose her three subjects to explore. There is a virtually unlimited range of possibilities from which she could have drawn. When you think of vulnerability and look at Amy's clue words above, you might select a little brook as your element of nature, a tiny minnow or a rabbit as an animal, and a long-stemmed crystal goblet as a man-made object—all are vulnerable amidst a threatening environment.

Amy, of course, came up with her own. "What popped into my head were a cloud, a butterfly, and a chiffon scarf," she said, before moving to a spot in the studio where she could immerse herself in a Combination Exploration, going from one subject to another as she was impelled.

Afterwards, she described her experience for us. It appeared that Amy had no trouble becoming a cloud at once:

> I was weightless, not happy exactly. More like content. I floated up high where everything was clean and lovely, away above everything that wasn't. I drifted on, content. Slowly my pure whiteness began to change into pure colors and my expanse became the wings of a butterfly. I was conscious of how beautiful I was. I wanted to alight on a daisy, but a breeze blew me to a buttercup. It didn't matter. I was so beautiful and the world was such a perfect place for butterflies. As I was drifting from flower to flower in the air, I became a ballerina. Floating, flying, soaring. The thought that I was deviating from the exercise requirements came fleetingly to my mind, but I didn't care. I allowed myself to go on. It was so joyful, so weightless. My arms were floating like a scarf. I consciously applied the scarf to my entire body. A silken, gauzy thing, so pretty. The breeze picked me up and puffed me up to the sky. I was soaring, twirling, laughing with pleasure. I danced across the sky in the sunlight and found I was a cloud again. The wind was colder now and the sun was gone. The wind was breaking me up and I was afraid. I became a scarf—one piece, whole. The wind sucked me down to earth and I caught on a thorn bush. I tried to pull free and I tore. I hurt. I went back to the butterfly and I struggled to tear loose, but my wing broke and I couldn't fly. I tried to become a cloud again, or a scarf, but I couldn't, and I was so afraid.

Amy's Exploration captured the essence of Blanche's character. It is also a model of how you can move between subjects organically.

While each subject was similar, the Exploration of each lead to some contrasting responses. Her broken cloud had different rhythms from her broken butterfly, which, again, differed from those of the torn scarf.

Her identification with Blanche's vulnerability will guide her to the nuances with which to play a scene. Amy's task was now to read *Streetcar* again and select one of Blanche's scenes or monologues to work on for the next session.

When Amy's class met next, she presented her work and she showed us a convincing, vulnerable Blanche. I reminded her that even as consistently vulnerable as she is throughout the play, Blanche, like all good characters, is complex and has more than one *self*. For instance, in her scenes with Mitch, when she dazzles him with her elegance, she is gay, charming, and confident in what she is doing. Is she being the *instinctive self*, automatically reacting to a man's admiration? Or is she momentarily the *social self*, consciously manipulating him for her own desperate ends? Or is she made up of both?

Her vulnerability underlies everything, but her other *selves* must be recognized where they are present. Otherwise, an actor runs the risk of playing a character too much on one note, even with the variety of shadings experienced in a full Exploration. First become secure with the dominant *self*, however, before moving on to work on the others.

WILLY LOMAN

I had one student actor who was very ambitious—he chose to work on Arthur Miller's Everyman, Willy Loman from *Death of a Salesman*. This isn't a role a younger man would normally select to study—even though Lee J. Cobb was only thirty-seven when he portrayed the battered salesman on Broadway in 1949.

Bill, to his credit, came up with an interesting interpretation. The following is the summary he read to the class:

> Sixty-three-year-old salesman Willy Loman returns to his Brooklyn home after an unsuccessful tour of his territory. In flashback, we see a younger, go-getter Willy, happy with his wife and two growing boys. Now Biff, the older son, who had caught Willy with another woman, has returned home after years of wandering aimlessly. Biff despises

his father, unlike his younger brother Happy. Willy's wife is helpless to change this and to persuade Willy he is not the failure he knows he is. Deep in a depression about every aspect of his life, Willy kills himself so that his wife can collect his insurance.

Bill's summary seemed cursory to me. He didn't mention significant events like Willy's getting fired, and he didn't seem to note Willy's favoritism toward Biff, though perhaps, from Willy's point of view, he treats both equally. This was Bill's list of clue words:

Trapped, futile, helpless, weak, incompetent, unrealistic, passive, fantasizing, blundering, bewildered, lost, stumbling, lonely, dependent, manic-depressive, defenseless, bumbling, tormented, panicky, hollow, uncertain, anonymous, blustery, overwhelmed.

When asked what dominant self Bill had chosen from this analysis, he said, "Vulnerable. Underneath all the bragging and fantasy and his wishful thinking, he's a scared, little man, as vulnerable as they come."

After Bill did his Tuning Up exercises, including a *vulnerable self* exercise, he told us his three subjects of Exploration and went off to explore. You'll notice from his account of the experience that he didn't start with his element of nature subject. Don't feel beholden to begin with your element just because it preceded the other subjects in this book. Start with whatever subject attracts you instinctively. Bill started with his animal:

I was a mouse. I was in a subway station and a train was pulling in. The noise was unbelievable, overwhelming. I went into a panic. Gigantic feet were all around me, running, stomping. I didn't know which way to go to avoid being trampled. None of the giants even knew I was there. I ran blindly, running, running.

Suddenly I was a newspaper, blowing in the draft of the departing train. I whirled and snapped in the wind, fragmenting, being blown in all directions. I was falling, being mangled and stepped on by wet, muddy feet. I had to escape. I was a mouse again, scampering desperately out of the station to the open air. Freedom! I became the newspaper, pulled up, up into the gray sky, and then falling, drifting downward.

I was snow—wet, heavy flakes that became water when I hit the pavement. I tried to turn into beautiful six-pointed crystals that lasted, but it was no use. Just big, fat, soggy flakes that turned into a puddle. Then I was the mouse again, drowning in the puddle. I was so frightened I became the newspaper, lying in the puddle, becoming smeared, a soggy lump of nothing that people stepped on and kicked aside. And nobody knew it was me.

Notice how Bill kept going back and forth between his subjects. He became a mouse several times, a newspaper a couple times, each occurrence deepening the physicalization. In this regard, Bill's Exploration was exemplary.

I've seen actors play Willy as slow, heavy, dragging—this was Cobb's interpretation. That would suggest a larger, more stolid animal. I asked Bill how he had conceived of the character as small and quick in his movements, like a mouse. Bill replied that he'd never seen the play, "But from what I read, I understood the character to be a wired-up, nervous, agitated, little man."

That reading, in my opinion, is as good in every respect as anyone else's—Dustin Hoffman's portrayal of Willy Loman on Broadway a few years earlier was similar to Bill's interpretation. Bill's next step was to keep the results of his Exploration in his scene work and he could be assured that his interesting interpretation would make itself evident.

To demonstrate how characters dominated by the *vulnerable self* can be extremely different, I asked Amy how Bill's vulnerability as Willy differed from hers as Blanche. It was obvious to her, "Blanche was dreamy, poetic, cultured, aristocratic. I could go on and on. Willy, on the other hand, was none of these. He was lower middle class. He didn't have her values."

When Bill brought in one of Willy's scenes for the next session, I found that the nervous, frightened little animal he chose in his Exploration worked very well. Although we laughed at times, the laughter was that of unease, which showed that we empathized with his anguish and vulnerability as Willy.

Vulnerability can be expressed in as many ways as there are well-written characters. Everybody has his or her own problems. What caused these problems in the first place, and how the character reacts to them in the second, is what makes each character unique.

Let's take some examples of vulnerability. Caliban, in Shakespeare's *The Tempest*, is Prospero's slave, completely powerless and subject to his master's whims. This is a very simple, very obvious form of vulnerability, and it gives the monster a moving, human quality.

Equally obvious is Laura Wingfield in Tennessee Williams' *The*

Glass Menagerie. Slightly deformed in her legs, she has let this physical flaw—which stronger persons would have placed in a different, less dominant perspective—cause her to retreat from life, to play with the little glass animals who share her fragility.

In Eugene O'Neill's *Long Day's Journey into Night,* Mary Tyrone, the mother, is vulnerable through her dependency on drugs. She had been a trusting, happy, young wife until incompetent medical treatment had made her an addict. Through her morphine habit she has become passive and helpless to control her life.

Not unlike this is the character of Lavinia in Lillian Hellman's *Another Part of the Forest.* Taking refuge in religion from a coarse, insensitive husband, Lavinia lives in her own world until she sees an opportunity to fulfill her dreams. On the other hand, as opposed to being a victim of fate, Shakespeare's King Lear created his own vulnerability by putting himself at the mercy of his two unscrupulous daughters. Othello fell prey to his own character flaws, which Iago understood and manipulated, altering the Moor's decisive character until he was helpless in the toils of his own passions.

Your study of the *vulnerable self* has enabled you to understand these characters on a deeply emotional level. No matter how varied these characters may appear, the clue words of your analysis will indicate the common basis these characters share. No matter how alike these characters are, your analysis and your Explorations will result in very different physicalizations.

14

Approaching Instinctive Roles

ROBERTA

Before the film *Moonstruck* brought national attention to the work of John Patrick Shanley, he had written a two-character play called *Danny and the Deep Blue Sea* that ran successfully for quite a while Off-Broadway in the early 1980s. One of my students decided to work on Roberta, a very dynamic character. Carol brought the following play summary into class:

> Thirty-one-year-old Roberta has a thirteen-year-old son who is cared for by her parents, whom she holds responsible for ruining her marriage. Unable to be alone with herself, she picks up twenty-nine-year-old Danny in a bar. She is attracted by his violent aura and, without necessarily being aware of it, hopes that he will hurt her so that she will be punished for having indulged in fellatio with her father. That way she hopes to be relieved of the guilt which has been destroying her. Instead, their love-making is mutually tender and protective. She accepts his proposal of marriage. The next morning Roberta tells Danny that the night meant nothing and she won't marry him. He understands her guilt and forgives it, as a priest would. Her tenderness has relieved him of the need to express himself through violence

and the play concludes with the implication that they will heal each other and grow into mature, loving individuals.

Carol did a good job of keeping the play summary focused on her character's point of view, describing those events that particularly influenced her behavior throughout the course of the play. Carol's clue words completed her analysis:

> Hating, bitter, resentful, guilt-ridden, limited, non-intellectual, brutal, direct, unafraid, physical, emotional, passionate, angry, hurt, vengeful, tender, compassionate, hard, lost, vulnerable, panicky, desperate, wounded, bold, trapped, yearning, unsatisfied, violent, restless, dangerous, alert, agitated, unpredictable, abrupt, menacing, turbulent.

From her summary and clue words Carol decided that Roberta's character was dominated by her *instinctive self*. I questioned whether she might have considered either the *unresolved* or *decisive self* because Roberta at different times exhibits characteristics of both. "Yes," Carol answered, "I had thought of them, but I decided they weren't right. All her actions, all her violence, grew out of her instincts. At every moment she behaved instinctively, reacting to each moment just as she felt."

Carol then did her Tuning Up exercises, as well as a Tuning In exercise from the *instinctive self* chapter, stimulating her sensory response. Having already chosen three subjects she went immediately into her Exploration, which turned out to be quite something. It almost wore me out just watching her. I don't know when I'd seen so much energy in an Exploration. I was afraid she'd collapse. I could sense Roberta's explosive violence in her. Even when she wasn't moving, I could feel the tension ready to erupt—excellent for the character. This is how she described her experience:

> I just wanted to be peaceful, to be let alone, never to do anything. I didn't want to move, but suddenly I ran, banging against the walls. I wanted to crush everybody around me, to bump them, to knock them over, but I was afraid to hurt someone. So I stood frozen in one place. Then I started to run again, banging against the walls, the columns. A terrible noise sounded in my head, banging, banging. A big bell. Running back and forth, banging. I was the clapper of the bell. I hurt. I could sense the powerful vibrations all over. Bang, bang. The sound was driving me crazy. I couldn't take it anymore. I wanted out. Out and away. I ran away from it. I broke free, soaring, wild, bright, explosive splash of energy splitting the sky. I was lightning. Powerful.

> Unbeatable. Angry. Immense anger. I leaped in all directions, blasting everything, burning everything. I was an animal, leaping, raging, afraid of nothing. Indestructible, savage. Wanting to kill, darting forward, sideways. A mongoose, killing, leaping, flashing here, there, into the clouds. I was exhausted but I couldn't stop. I was hurting, but I was still angry, banging against the walls.

I applauded the power and size of Carol's experience in the Exploration and hoped that she would be able to maintain it in her scene. In the next session we had together, the violence in Carol's scene was very convincing. It was the brutal, resentful, vengeful character of the first act's instinctive Roberta. Now that that part of the role's physicality was firmly under her belt, I suggested she work on a scene in which Roberta expresses tenderness.

LEE

This is the role that first brought John Malkovich to the attention of New York audiences. The Steppenwolf Theatre Company from Chicago brought Sam Shepard's play *True West* to New York in 1983, and the show was later filmed for public television. There are two good roles for young men, and one of my students wanted to work on Lee. This is Dan's summary:

> Lee, a semi-literate, hulking desert rat, who supports himself by stealing household appliances and other valuables, drops in at his mother's home. He finds her away and his well-educated brother Austin housesitting while he finishes up a film script he has all but sold. Lee bullies and torments the slighter Austin and wins a bet that compels the producer to buy his idea for a screenplay instead of Austin's. At first, Lee tries to force Austin to write it for him. However, bit by bit, the brothers find themselves in a role reversal. Lee now wants to complete the script, and bribes his brother into helping him by promising to teach Austin how to live in the desert. The mother's return to her house, which the brothers' swilling and vandalism have turned into a shambles, brings matters to a head. Lee goads Austin too far and the worm turns. Austin tries to strangle Lee, but the latter pulls himself to his feet and the two confront each other tensely as the play ends.

Dan's summary is pretty complete, as you can see if you're familiar with the play. He does leave out any mention whatsoever of their father, who was a pretty big factor in the two brother's subsequent psychology. Dan's clue words for Lee then lead him to his choice of self:

> Violent, abusive, spontaneous, treacherous, self-centered, hostile, bullying, shrewd, vicious, stubborn, passionate, careless, selfish, brutal, manipulative, loner, destructive, primitive, explosive, powerful, angry, dangerous, self-pitying, menacing, mysterious, determined, non-conforming, rebellious, amoral, asocial, unpredictable, futile, damned.

Dan's first feeling about Lee was that he was purely instinctive, "He does whatever he pleases, without caring who gets hurt or loses out—just as long as it's not him." Dan paused, then went on, however, to say, "The more I think about it, the more contradictions I find. How can an instinctive character be so manipulative, so devious, as Lee is in trying to get what he wants?"

Another actor in the same class elaborated, "Lee saw only what was in front of him and he reacted accordingly, crashing in where there was an opening, pulling back when he felt threatened. To me, none of this is incompatible with the *instinctive self.*" Dan then did his Tuning Up exercise, an *instinctive self* exercise, and went into his Exploration. This is how he described it to us afterwards:

> I curled up like a ball. I was uncomfortable. I jumped to my feet. I ran from one side of the room to the other, back and forth, bouncing off the wall, almost knocking some of the people over. I couldn't stop myself. I was a billiard ball. I rolled in all different directions. I screamed. I was thunder. I was so angry. I stalked around, holding tight, drawing deep breaths until I let them go with earth-shaking shrieks. I shrieked again and again, and I was pounding my chest. I was a gorilla. I was filled with rage, but then I was curious about where I was and I looked around. Exploring. I found a tree with fruit, so I ate some. I stepped on a snake. I jumped away fast. I got angry and I pounded my chest and screamed. I rolled on the floor. I made a noise. I came up against another billiard ball and I smacked it hard. I was thunder. I walked around, making everything afraid when I let go. I was euphoric. I loved it. It was fun.

Dan's scene, like Carol's, managed to contain much of the violence that he'd discovered through his Exploration. But I should make an important point here. Just because Carol and Dan both chose to play the violence in their instinctive characters doesn't mean that is the only instinctive quality to explore. True, there are other instinctive characters filled with violence—latent or active. Stanley Kowalski, who puts the finishing touches on Blanche's madness in *Streetcar*, is one. Unlike the others however, Stanley is motivated by contempt for what he perceives as Blanche's pretensions. He acts instinctively to destroy what he has no use for.

Romeo and Juliet are a different case. All their instincts are concentrated on their love for each other. Their instinctive drive for immediate action disregards consequences. Everything is justified. Nothing matters but their love. The ensuing violence is not inherent in their natures. It happens. It is not what they want. Their tender, generous, giving, loving instincts betray them into tragedy.

15

Approaching Social Roles

ARSINOË

Molière, the great 17th century French playwright, wrote some wonderful comedies, containing good classical roles for women. Richard Wilbur's bright, buoyant translations have particularly helped bring Molière's work back onto the English-speaking world's stages. Emily chose to work on Arsinoë, a supporting character in *The Misanthrope*. This is how she summarized the play:

> Arsinoë is a fashionable lady of the court in 17th century France. Under the guise of friendship, she visits Célimène, ostensibly to warn her about gossip in which the latter figures, but actually to give herself the pleasure of spitefully passing on in as hurtful a way as possible whatever she had heard—or invented. Also as a friend, Arsinoë flatters Alceste, the man in love with Célimène, and tries to destroy the attachment with an eye to acquiring him for herself. When this falls through, she hastily denies any interest in him.

Emily's synopsis perfectly adheres to the requirements that the summation be from the character's perspective. She has neatly encapsulated only those important plot points that would be of interest to Arsinoë. Then she read us her clue words:

> Hypocritical, two-faced, bitchy, catty, self-serving, spiteful, jealous, envious, man-hungry, destructive, vulnerable, desperate, single-minded, lying, disappointed, worldly, silly, needing, falsely pious, disloyal, priggish, smug, condescending, censorious, sour, sophisticated, vain, busybody, judgmental, unrealistic, straitlaced, fading, frightened.

Emily had no hesitation naming which of the six *selves* most dominated Arsinoë's character. "The *social self*—no doubt about it. Social through and through—everything she does is behind her social mask," Emily said. She then proceeded to her Tuning Up exercises, including a masking exercise from Chapter 4. After her Exploration, she told of the following experience:

> I saw the other people. They seemed to be having fun. It made me miserable, angry. I couldn't stand them. I hissed and spat at them and dirty yellow paint came out of me—I was a can of spray paint. One of the people was laughing. I was sure he was laughing at me. I wanted to vomit. I went up to him and sprayed paint all over him. It made me feel good. I pranced from one to another, spraying everybody. They were looking at me. I was important. I was beautiful. I wanted everyone to see me. I was a peacock. I squawked and preened myself and my neck was shining blue-green. I strutted, circling the room so everyone could see how beautiful I was. Every now and then someone wouldn't get out of my way and I hissed and sprayed them with yellow paint. I wanted to stretch. I spread my wings and flew up. I was higher than everyone. There was nothing I couldn't do. I could fix all of them. I was rain. Not quite rain—a drizzle, cold, persistent. I dripped down their necks, streaked their glasses, spoiled their hair, ruined their shoe-shines. I made them uncomfortable. I liked it like that.

Arsinoë doesn't have many scenes, but those she does have are great. I was looking forward to what Emily would do with one during the next session.

Working on this character provides an insightful context for the examination of the *social self*. What has created her *social self*? Arsinoë is not two-dimensional. You might want to consider what makes her *social self* interesting. Why is her *social self* so vitriolic? Is it simply that she wants other women's beauty, youth, men, riches? Or is it that her *vulnerable self* is crying out somewhere under the mask to be loved or pitied or cherished? Think of how Arsinoë can be aristocratic and vulgar at the same time—self-assured and hurting, venomous and pitiful. There's a lot of humanity compressed in her short scenes. Again, it is important to remember that fully-developed, believable characters can't be simplified and reduced to one-dimensional *selves*. The dominant *self* and unique characteristics play themselves out through various modes of expression, and are acted upon by complex sets of circumstances.

IAGO

Throughout the last few centuries, many renowned actors who were asked to take on the title role of Shakespeare's tragedy, *Othello*, have been loath to do so for one reason—Iago steals the show. The conniving, manipulating soldier is one of Shakespeare's greatest dramatic creations. Frank decided he wanted to take a shot at it. This is the summary which he devised from his readings of the play:

> Iago, an officer in Othello's army, has been passed over for promotion. He plots to destroy everyone who has come between him and his ambition. While pretending to be loyal, he manipulates Othello's unsuspecting nature until Othello kills his innocent wife in a rage of jealousy. Along the way, Iago murders fellow officers, destroys his own wife, and finally himself in achieving his full revenge.

Frank's summation is about as succinct as possible. He could have gone a little further into detail and thereby supplied himself with more evidence with which to make a decision about the dominant *self*. As it is, it seems he's already made up his mind before he wrote his synopsis. These are the clue words Frank listed:

> Jealous, envious, suave, ambitious, passionate, ashamed, wounded, proud, festering, hating, violent, destructive, vengeful, devious, indirect, patient, manipulative, poisonous, extreme, fanatic, intelligent, fastidious, unscrupulous, conscienceless, daring, confident, self-righteous, callous, sly, determined, ruthless, perceptive.

As I had suspected, Frank was pretty clear about which *self* he'd decided Iago was, "I don't think there's any doubt about Iago's being a *social self*," he told us. "The archetypal *social self* if ever there was one."

One actor disagreed and brought up an interesting point. It seemed to her, from her knowledge of the play, that Iago could be just as equally dominated by his *decisive self.* Her rationale was that, "from the outset he knew exactly what he wanted to do and he went right ahead and did it."

Another classmate came to Frank's defense, stating that Iago's "decisiveness was hidden behind a mask. In his scenes with Othello, Roderigo, and the other characters, all his dealings were sneaky and underhanded. Even with his wife."

Soon this discussion became a free-for-all. One actor chimed in that because Iago was always "open with the audience" and never held anything back, he was a perfect *trusting self* in the way he confided his plans, almost inviting the audience to participate.

But Dan strongly disagreed: "Even with the audience, he is still the manipulator." And of course another actor felt that Iago was dominated by his *vulnerable self.* "If he hadn't been so vulnerable, he wouldn't have been so hurt by being passed over, and he wouldn't have had such a great need for revenge," this actor asserted.

I agreed, however, with Frank, who had the last word on this occasion since he was the one working on the character. "I see him as devious and manipulative primarily, lying to everyone. He's honest with himself. He knows what he's doing, but he wears a mask the rest of the time. I can't see him as anything but social, and that's the way I'd play him."

The discussion we had, at times heated, proves how multifaceted and complex Iago's character is, and this is what makes him a challenging part to act. I told the other actors that if any of them conceived of Iago differently, as being another self in some of his scenes, then they should play him the way they see him. But over all, I strongly believe that this character is dominated by the *social self.*

With such a wonderfully rich and complex character, the choice of subjects is even more crucial. Which element embodies Iago's *social self*? Is it darkness, which covers the earth the way Iago's suave exterior covers his inner treachery? Is it a volcano, repressing the violence inherent in his nature until the catastrophic release?

Which animal embodies the same spirit as the element of nature? The boa constrictor, winding around Othello, entangling him, engulfing him? Or perhaps the spider, creating the web that traps the unsuspecting Moor? What about a leopard lurking in a tree? Which man-made object? A blanket, concealing what it overlies? A pillow, appearing to be an item of comfort, but that can be used to smother? Select your subjects carefully.

Frank's subsequent Tuning Up and *social self* exercise from Chapter 4 led to his Exploration, which he describes below:

> In the beginning I lay on the floor quietly, feeling that I was the earth, feeling deep below the earth. But I wasn't really quiet. Inside I began to feel tense, uncomfortable. The tension grew and I felt I could fall apart if I didn't hold on to myself. I curled up into a ball and wrapped my arms around my legs, holding as tightly as I could. The pressures were piling up. I was trembling with the urge to rid myself of them, but I held on tightly. I screamed when the slow, relentless pressure continued to mount. I screamed again, but I held on. Some part of me said, "Not yet. Not yet."
>
> Suddenly I was free, relaxed. I was a shark sliding through the water, cool against my skin. My tail waved back and forth, propelling me through the black ocean. I was looking for something. Hunting. I was hungry. So hungry. I knew I would find it and when I did it would be helpless against me. I knew it would take me a while to find my prey and I was growing ravenous, but I was willing to wait. How much better my meal would be for the waiting . . .
>
> Waiting . . . I was waiting under a tree. I was a steel trap with open jaws, waiting. Unsatisfied. I had been created for a purpose. I didn't know what, but I was empty and couldn't be satisfied yet. But I knew it would happen if I waited. I lay under the tree, quietly. I curled into the ball, not so quiet.
>
> Then the pressures inside me were growing intense again. Hot. Demanding. They were more than I could bear. I cracked open. I was an earthquake, exploding, smashing everything around me. In a great rush of freedom I darted forward and caught my prey in my jaws. But I was the steel trap also, snapping my teeth around my prey. As the shark and as the trap, I relished the agonies of my helpless prey. I was complete at last.

I found Frank's Exploration to be extremely good, physical work for Iago. He then went on to reread the play and select a scene in which he would try to use some of the physicality he discovered in his Exploration.

Arsinoë and Iago both have qualities of viciousness under their masks, but this trait is not a necessary component of the *social self*. Let's take two examples. Ben Jonson's title character in one of his comedies, *Volpone*, pretends to be dying. He fleeces his greedy hangers-on, tricking them into giving him gifts they hope will influence his choice of beneficiaries. They are, without exception, scoundrels. Played as farce, Volpone's avarice has an almost innocent quality.

James M. Barrie's *Admirable Crichton* goes in another direction. As a servant who runs a household with efficiency behind his mask of professionalism, he is ordered about or ignored by the master and daughters of the house. When the yacht on which they are all embarked is wrecked, only Crichton has the wits and ability to enable the marooned party to survive. His erstwhile master deems it an honor to serve him, and the ladies vie for his favors. He is the uncontested king of the island until a passing vessel rescues them. Crichton again becomes the perfect, deferential servant, his temporary ascendancy a thing of the forgotten past.

16

Approaching
Trusting Roles

NORA

Perhaps no character in dramatic history is more known for a decisive action than that with which Nora Helmer ends Ibsen's masterpiece, *A Doll's House*. It is often said that when Nora walks out on her family at the end of the play, the slamming door was heard around the world. Many consider this action—absolutely a mindboggling, revolutionary choice for a respectable 19th century Norwegian woman—to mark the beginning of modern drama.

Of course, Nora is a role many of my students find impossible to resist. But because of Nora's abrupt change in character, I told Mary to concentrate on the Nora that is evident in the largest part of the play, up to the point where she realizes Torvald will not stand by her. I warned her that the ending can be misleading as to what *self* she is predominantly. Mary summarized the play as follows:

> Nora Helmer, young wife of Torvald and mother of two children is happy in her small world. Its first crack appears when a clerk in Torvald's bank blackmails her with a check she had forged many years before, when she had found no other way to help her ailing

husband. Her world splits asunder when Torvald, on discovering her crime, blasts her. Until then, Nora had believed that his love was so great he would gladly assume her guilt himself, instead of castigating her for ruining his career. Although the blackmail threat dissipates harmlessly, the damage has been done. Nora realizes she has been a doll in a doll's house, to be played with and caressed when all is well—not a marriage partner. She leaves to make a life for herself where she can respect herself and earn the respect of others.

This summation is very strongly from Nora's point of view. Imagine what Torvald's synopsis would read like! It would be completely different in tone, with a conflicting reading of the events. The only question I might have is with the last sentence. Ibsen doesn't make clear the reason Nora leaves. Mary has made up her mind, though, which is fine. Here is Mary's list of clue words and phrases:

Joyous, confiding, loving, confident, relaxed, assured, open, safe, content, secure, caring, devoted, nurturing, catering, supportive, sees the best in everyone, warm, generous, self-sacrificing, charming, intelligent, sensitive, loyal, active, gentle, innocent, imaginative.

These clues lead Mary to choose the *trusting self* as Nora's dominant aspect. As she told me, "Nora is so open, so giving. She's a really special, very nice person. I really like her." Unlike my contentious class in the last chapter, none of her fellow actors disputed her analysis. Mary's Tuning Up and *trusting self* exercises lead her to the following experience in her Exploration:

I lay on the floor, thinking about how I love my family. Suddenly I couldn't lie still anymore. I had to do something about the feelings that were choking me with happiness. I jumped to my feet, running madly around, bounding with joy. I was a dog, so glad someone had come home. I ran and jumped, with my tongue hanging out. I rolled over and over on the ground and jumped up and down until I became tired. I stopped to rest, and I became a flower. I turned my face to the sun and opened my petals so that the bees could reach my pollen. I danced in the breeze that caressed me. How lovely it was to feel the air against every part of me, to accept its embrace. How delicious the moist earth was to my feet. I lay down and I wasn't a flower. I was a warm, cuddly blanket. I spread out like a carpet, I folded and unfolded, covering, caressing everything I passed. I reveled in the comfort I was providing, enjoying my soft fleeciness, the perfume I was providing for everyone's pleasure. Perfume? I was the flower, giving my beauty to everyone. I was the dog, basking in the glow of people who loved me.

Mary's Exploration seemed all right except for the beginning. I asked her why was she thinking about Nora's family—her family—when her mind should have been clear as she lay on the floor in neutral. She told me that since she had just read the play, she couldn't disconnect herself from it. When she was on the floor, she couldn't wait to do something about Nora, to get into her, "I felt strong identification with her, so I made the decision not to fight my feelings and to see wherever they would take me."

Obviously, her feelings took her to good places because her Exploration was very interesting. She said she couldn't wait to get into Nora. The truth is, she was invaded by her character before she started the exercise. It was Nora who led Mary into action.

I wasn't surprised at the conviction she brought to Nora later, when she did her scene work. Her Nora was consistent, graceful, and confident. We sensed the strong emotional link between her own and Nora's truth.

We've discussed before how your clue words lead you into the character, and how different clue words will guide you to different physicalizations, even when the roles in question might be considered as being the same *self*. Take the title character of George Bernard Shaw's *Saint Joan* as a case in point. This was a young woman, only a few years younger than Nora, but an inhabitant of 15th century France rather than 19th century Norway. You could conclude that her unswerving determination to drive the English from the sacred soil of France makes her a decisive character, and you would be right. However, remember that all her actions were motivated by her utter faith in her "voices"—her instructions from the Saints Catherine, Margaret, and Michael. We see that her decisiveness is an outgrowth of something more basic—her *trusting self*.

In playing Joan and in playing Nora you might choose this same *self* as the dominant one for each character, even though one woman is concerned with saving her country and the other with running a happy home. Joan lays down the law to king, generals, prelates, and others, while Nora sweetly caters to her family. Yet it would be obvious to the actor working on these two roles that these two trusting lives would be interpreted very differently in their physicalization.

LENNY

Rarely does a novel translate so beautifully to the dramatic form as does John Steinbeck's *Of Mice and Men*, a heart-rending tale of two ranch workers drifting through the American West. George S. Kaufman, better known as the playwright of such classic American comedies as *You Can't Take It with You*, directed the first Broadway production in 1937. More recently, in the early 1970s, James Earl Jones' critically acclaimed portrayal of Lenny reintroduced Steinbeck's play to a new generation of theatergoers. Sam, who decided he wanted to portray Lenny, came to class with the following summary:

> Lenny, somewhat retarded, trusts and obeys George, upon whom he is completely dependent. The two itinerant workers are constantly on the run because Lenny's immense strength, which he cannot control, frightens young girls who misunderstand his desire to caress soft, pretty things, like their skirts or hair. It grieves him that he destroys the mice and puppies he wants only to pet. In a new job, Lenny accidentally kills a farm wife and flees. George finds him and distracts him with their favorite story of how the two will have their own home someday. While Lenny is happily daydreaming, George shoots him in the back of the head.

Sam's summary was to the point, except that the character, Lenny, wouldn't know that George shoots him. Sam must know because he read the play. This type of situation often occasions a frequent problem for actors—anticipation. If the actor playing Lenny gives any hint that he knows what's coming, the audience won't be as affected by his death. Luckily, by using your analysis and clue words to choose a dominant *self*, and three subjects to explore, you should discover enough of a physical and emotional life so that you become too involved *being* the character to anticipate the end result. These are the clue words Sam selected:

> Slow, dazed, trusting, hopeful, loving, kind, dependent, obedient, gentle, caring, blundering, optimistic, loyal, hurt, powerful, humble, frightened, inarticulate, clumsy, unaware, awkward, credulous, sluggish, ashamed.

Lenny's dominant *self* would seem obvious—the *trusting self*. The character is completely trusting, absolutely relying on George for guidance in every aspect of his life. When I asked Sam what he thought, he agreed completely, "Lenny is the most uncomplicated character I've ever come across—the *trusting self* is so overwhelming, there's practically no other one." However, one could make a case for Lenny's having strong characteristics of the *vulnerable* and *instinctive selves.*

Sam went with his own choice, naturally enough, and after Tuning Up and completing an exercise from Chapter 5 went into his Exploration. This is his account of the experience:

> I lay on the floor until I could feel the power surging through my whole body. In my engine, my wheels. I was a locomotive. It felt good. I was happy going full throttle along the tracks, because I knew people were depending on me and I was doing a good job. I ran around and around the room in wide circles, at an even steady pace, and I knew I would never get tired. And I was content. Then, without my wanting to, I could feel my pace slowing down and becoming erratic, and then my wheels stopped. I tried to move but I was rooted to the ground. I felt I was letting everyone down and they wouldn't like me anymore. I was stuck and I couldn't run. I stretched out my arms and I was a tree. A big, powerful tree with wide branches. I stood tall and the sun was warm and my leaves quivered in the breeze, and my roots and trunk were strong in the earth, and it was wonderful to be a tree. I wanted to shelter the whole world. One of my branches started to crack and I tried to hold my arms up, but it broke off and it dropped to the ground and smashed everything it landed on. I felt very bad and I wanted to run away, and I ran and ran until I was a rhinoceros, and everything in my way got broken, and I couldn't stop running, and I ran and ran until I had to stop and I was an engine again, stalled on the track, and everyone was angry with me.

From this Exploration, Sam found all sorts of emotional and physical life with which to imbue Lenny. It was very interesting to see how in Sam's performance the *trusting self* went hand-in-hand with the *vulnerable*. His Lenny trusted completely. He was open, exposed, defenseless. As the audience, we participated in his danger, of which he was unaware. It was a very moving scene.

While Lenny trusted George one hundred percent, his inarticulate faith did not extend much beyond that. He knew the rest of the world could be angry and punishing, and he relied on George to keep him safe.

No *trusting self* could be more trusting than Elwood P. Dowd, from Mary Chase's comedy *Harvey.* With his sharp edges gently blurred by a slight alcoholic haze, Elwood, who never met a man he didn't like, routinely invited home to dinner everyone he met—taxi driver, barfly, doctor. It never occurred to him that any of the people he picked up might do harm. He expected nothing but kindness and did not recognize the existence of danger.

17

Approaching Unresolved Roles

MISS JULIE

This short play is one of August Strindberg's most well-known. The great Swedish dramatist, infamous for his misogynist tendencies, nevertheless created, especially in *Miss Julie*, solid, meaty roles for women. In many ways, they're more interesting than the male roles. Susan, a student firmly of the 20th century told me she really wanted to call the character "*Ms*. Julie." This is her summary:

> Miss Julie is the proud daughter of a once-great house. She has been brought up oddly, according to the society of 1888 and today. Her mother, a radical feminist, created sexual identity confusion in Julie's mind. Julie adored her father, even while she believed the female to be the superior of the sexes. Suddenly succumbing to passion on Midsummer's Eve, Julie allows herself to be seduced by an ambitious, manipulative manservant. Overwhelmed by his masculinity, she loses confidence in the ideas on which she has built her life. She loses the ability to make decisions—whether to stay, assert her authority, and pretend nothing has happened, or whether to run away alone or with the servant, Jean. She has disgraced her class, demeaned herself, lost her sexual identity and her independence, and become subservient to

a menial. She can't even determine whether to live or die and finally accepts Jean's suggestion that she kill herself.

As is evident from Susan's summary, the character changes radically through the course of the play. The choice of *self* is not so obvious as in previous instances. Susan's list of clue words and phrases shows the range of characteristics Julie exhibits from beginning to end:

Confident, self-assured, bewildered, desperate, terrified, proud, betrayed, passionate, unconventional, impetuous, sensual, confused, intelligent, gullible, dependent, vacillating, topsy-turvy, elegant, unruly, unrestrained, haughty, crushed, flirtatious, decadent, teasing, taunting, despairing, lost, daring, manipulated.

When I asked Susan which *self* she was going to choose for this extremely complex character, she seemed to waver at first. She saw Julie as "very authoritative in the beginning and very confident in her superiority over Jean." At this stage Susan thought Julie was decisive. "But," she continued, "almost immediately, we realize how her servant is manipulating her, and she is very vulnerable. The situation got out of hand. Everything she had built her life on had collapsed. She was as helpless as a baby. She was unable, really unable, to make any decision. At this point, she had nothing left to serve as a compass. Everything she had believed in—everything she had trusted was gone. Whichever decision she made could be wrong."

Some of my male students were having a hard time with Susan's interpretation. Dan asked Susan, "You're trying to say that among all her alternatives she couldn't find one that would work? I don't believe that."

Susan retorted, "Of course you don't. You're a man. You don't understand how important the loss of her sexual confidence was to her."

"I think you're making too much about it," Dan replied.

Emily supported Susan's premise, "I think that is one of the main causes for her not to be able to decide anything."

The discussion ended with Susan more convinced than ever—Julie "couldn't be more the *unresolved self.*" After her decision she went through her Tuning Up exercises and tried one of the unresolved situations from Chapter 6. Having already chosen her three subjects for Exploration, she went right into it. This is her description of the experience:

I rolled on the floor over to the wall, and then I rolled back again. I repeated this again and again. I became dizzy. I was a wave and every time I hit the wall I broke up, splashing and shattering. My body hurt. I was exhausted. I wanted to be something else. I tore loose from the floor and flew free. I was a bee. There was a red flower below me and I buzzed over to it. I started to load up with pollen. I saw a buttercup. I flew toward it but then the red flower looked more attractive. But I liked the buttercup too. I flew back and forth, unable to choose. Red . . . yellow . . . red . . . yellow. I knew I was stupid and it made me angry. Just pick one—red *or* yellow! I was red and yellow, a neon sign blinking. I was jerking red . . . yellow. I tried to stay red, very hard. I was the bee hovering over the red flower. A thorn on the red flower pierced me. I rolled on the ground in agony, and I was the wave, going back and forth.

This Exploration was full. It is noteworthy for how she begins with a subject, moves on to explore another, and then finds herself returning to a previous subject. In the case of her wave, it seemed that when she came back to it her emotional state had changed and so the physical expression of the element took on a new dimension.

Somehow Susan's eventual interpretation of Julie's unresolved aspect, though effective, didn't go far enough. She let her be too sweet in her characterization. She tilted a lot toward vulnerability. That's fine at times, of course. But she'd overlooked Julie's position. Julie was not without authority, not without power.

It was significant that she chose the bee in her Exploration. A bee has power in her sting. If Julie had exercised even the suggestion of a sting through her authority over Jean, this would have added yet another dimension, a strength to her interpretation.

I suggested a way of handling this problem which should serve as an example of how you work on many different roles. I proposed that she break up her very long scenes, isolating those in which Julie is indecisive from those in which she believed vulnerability was paramount. I told Susan to work on each section separately. Because Julie is lost between two worlds, her lack of resolution underlies everything—including her vulnerability.

Try breaking up any long scenes you may encounter in your own acting work, dividing the material into sections that seem dominated by different *selves*. Then explore different subjects and *self* exercises appropriate to each section, discovering new possibilities for the physicalization of your character. See if it doesn't work for you.

LOPAKHIN

Almost all of Russian dramatist Anton Chekhov's characters might seem unresolved—take the titular *Three Sisters,* for example, who are always talking of moving to Moscow, but who never leave. Chris decided to try Chekhov's budding capitalist Lopakhin from the play *The Cherry Orchard.* This is how he summarized the play:

> Lopakhin, now a well-to-do landowner, never forgets that the land he owns was worked by his father as a peasant. He is aware that the neighboring Ranevsky estate is in serious financial trouble and he wants to help, partly because he likes the Ranevsky family and partly because he is in love with Varya, the elder daughter of the house. Lopakhin advises them how to salvage their house and at least part of the cherry orchard on the estate—but they pay no attention. Although he knows Varya returns his love and he wants very much to propose the marriage everyone expects, he cannot bring himself to make the offer. The house and cherry orchard are inevitably lost. Lopakhin buys the estate, and although he is now able to keep Varya in her old home, he still can't bring himself to propose. Varya, waiting vainly for him to speak, leaves as the family breaks up and moves away.

Chris has obviously chosen a rich character, with an affecting past. He then complemented his summarization with his list of clue words:

> Gentle, kind, big, strong, shy, shrewd, caring, sincere, unpretentious, honest, loyal, trustworthy, competent, intelligent, practical, far-sighted, determined, wavering, hesitant, timid, not-daring, emotional, longing, insecure, rational, direct, serious, active, physical, unsure, striving, persistent, relentless, proud, inferior, awkward, able, flexible, responsive, protective.

For this study, I asked Chris to concern himself with Lopakhin's relationship to Varya. There was little doubt in his mind that this part of the character was dominated by the *unresolved self.* He preceded to do his Tuning Up exercises, finishing by trying one of the exercises from the chapter on the *unresolved self.* His Exploration, which he describes below, is a good example of how you must try not to "think" but *become* your subjects and let their energies drive you:

> I was an elephant, a leader elephant. I was large and strong. I walked through the trees, waving my trunk. I stepped over any little creatures in my way. A huge log lay across the path. I pushed it to one side so that the rest of the herd wouldn't have to step over it. A little calf came

up to me and I let him play between my legs. I was happy that everyone depended on my strength and judgment. I felt danger. I trum-
peted a signal for everyone to run. I brought up the rear, making sure
everyone was safe. I ran on and on. I was a piece of farm equipment—
a big machine. I ran smoothly down the even rows, cutting the grain,
threshing it, binding the stalks, piling them in neat little heaps. I was
competent. I was sure of what I was doing. I ran. I was becoming
uncomfortable. Was I really doing my best? How did I know? Was I
supposed to do something else? What? I started to think about it and
I had to stop the exercise.

In order to get back into the Exploration again, I decided to
become the elephant. I tried to think of a situation. It didn't work. So I
just stood there and let myself feel like the elephant. It felt awkward.
I was afraid to move. I panicked. I forced myself to walk and I fell. I
rolled down a slope. Falling, rolling, I came down with a splash. I was
a waterfall—a great cascade of white water—strong, determined.
Positive. Enjoying my power as branches were swept along in my
torrent, spinning in the whirlpool at my feet. Spinning, until I picked
them up and let them escape into the quiet water just beyond. It filled
all the depressions at my feet and continued to fall, always falling, yet
always the same, always the same. I stood up. I was the elephant, not
knowing what to do.

Besides the break in concentration I already noted, it seems obvious
that the elephant was giving Chris a hard time as a subject. He stated,
"It felt awkward" and the last line reaffirms this feeling of "not knowing what to do." I told him it was all right to feel "awkward" as the
character, but in his case, as the actor, it seemed to continually lead
him toward self-consciousness. When that happens, I suggested he
pick another subject and move on.

Lopakhin is a deceptive character. Here we have a man who,
throughout the play, proves himself to be decisive—a visionary with
his feet on the ground. By his own efforts he has raised himself from
the lowly status into which he was born to a position of affluence and
prestige in the community. He can see problems clearly and devise
effective means of dealing with them. A case in point: the development scheme to save the Ranevsky estate. Why then is this individual,
successful in every other aspect of his life, as unable to propose to a
woman who loves him as Hamlet, the archetypal *unresolved self*, is to
slay his father's murderer?

Chris had his own interpretation: "Basically, I think that underneath all the trappings of success, real as they are, Lopakhin is a

humble, insecure man. He can never forget his origins. No matter how welcome he is in the homes of the aristocracy, he is never completely comfortable. His peasant father is always looking over his shoulder, so to speak. Always reminding him he is in the presence of his betters."

As to his feelings about proposing, Chris believed that "Lopakhin really loves Varya, but he has put her on a pedestal. Even though he knows she would step down for him, he doesn't believe he is worthy of her, and as much as he wants to, he can't bring himself to propose."

In the final analysis, Chekhov doesn't give any specific reasons for Lopakhin's lack of resolution, but Chris's interpretation is valid. There are other possibilities also, but in this instance, his own instincts and logic have led him to a strong, credible characterization.

Chekhov's plays are full of characters who, at first glance, would seem to be unresolved. The characters in *The Cherry Orchard* are typical in many respects. Let's take a look at Madam Ranevsky, who owns the estate. Her decision—or lack of it—is the pivotal factor which determines the course of the play and the direction the lives of the characters will take. She doesn't decide. Her inertia makes the decision for her. But in this case, she is not indecisive. She simply refuses to recognize that a problem exists. Therefore, no decision has to be made. There is no struggle, no being torn between extremes, no agonizing. Disaster, when it comes, has no connection in her mind with her refusal to take action. She feels in no way responsible. It is just another unfortunate act of God, like a hailstorm or an earthquake.

When you look for the dominant *self* with which to identify a character, search for the subtleties that will show you the character's soul. It's important to look at the whole character and not be misled by an easy judgment or superficial indication.

18

Approaching
Decisive Roles

MEDEA

The central role in Euripides' *Medea* is a part that offers many traps.
Her passion, coupled with the epic sweep of the script, often leads to
overacting, and yet one can't easily get away with a simple, naturalis-
tic approach either. Those of us lucky enough to have seen Zoe Cald-
well's Broadway performance in 1982 glimpsed the possibility of
success. Nancy was determined to try her hand, however, and she
came to class with a synopsis, clue words, and subjects picked out.
This is her summary:

> Before the play begins, the sorceress Medea, Princess of Colchis, has
> betrayed her family and killed her brothers for love of the adventurer
> who had come seeking their treasure, the Golden Fleece. Medea flees
> to Corinth with Jason and the Fleece. She bears him two sons.
>   When the play opens, she learns that Jason plans to marry King
> Creon's daughter and take the boys from her. Medea contrives a
> hideous death for Creon and the girl and then, to revenge herself fur-
> ther on Jason, kills their children, whom she loves—but not so much as
> she now hates their father. She escapes to Athens, leaving Jason a bro-
> ken man.

Notice how Nancy's summary had to begin before the play itself, including history pertinent to her character's action? Don't forget to include such description in your summary when it is necessary.

Moving on to Nancy's clue words, she offered the following list. Observe how similar most of the words are:

> Focused, obsessed, intense, seething, hissing, snarling, raging, violent, shattering, puking, burning, immoderate, driving, forceful, passionate, popping, explosive, limitless, virulent, crushing, poisonous, squeezing, destructive, blind, indifferent to consequences, relentless, unbending, unstoppable, irresistible, unquenchable, immense.

Nancy didn't waver in her choice of dominant *self*. "Decisive. Definitely decisive," she insisted. I asked her if she had considered that possibly in Medea's hatred and compulsion for revenge she might have been the *instinctive self*.

Nancy had indeed contemplated the possibility. "Medea's instinct might have triggered the action," she replied, "but there was nothing instinctive in the way she carried out her plans. They were thought through in every detail and carried out in calculated, cold blood. I see her as decisive all the way."

And with that affirmation Nancy began her Tuning Up exercises. She complemented the twenty to thirty minutes of centering, release, and ignition work with a *decisive self* exercise. She then lay down and began her Exploration. She didn't remain prone very long, however. This is how she described it:

> I tried to lie still on the floor, but I couldn't. I was so suffused with energy I had to stand up and fling my arms wide—I was a hurricane and I ran through the room. I wanted to smash everyone in my way and I had to restrain myself from knocking the other people down or hitting them. I ran and ran, filled with rage, growing more angry as I tore around. Now my shape was changing—I had two long tiger legs and a tail that flew straight out behind me. I could feel my claws tucked in their sheaths, and the strength in my muscles. I was bounding now as I ran, leaping to the rhythm of my anger. Bounding. Bounding. My rage was focused, centered. I didn't know on what, but I knew I would get it, and anything that was in my way as well. Nothing could stop me.
>
> I stopped running and took a deep breath of anger and walked tightly and carefully around the jungle. Suddenly I could bear it no longer, being held in, and I was exploding as dynamite in a wild scream that became the howl of the hurricane, rushing to destroy. The

fury inside me grew and grew until I exploded again. It felt right to smash everything around me and I spun with delight until I was exhausted. I sank down as the tiger, tired, but at peace at last.

Nancy seemed to discover a range of physicality in her Exploration— moving from controlled, focused movements to limitless passion. This boded well for her work on a scene in *Medea*. She managed to avoid the common pitfalls, and despite Medea's being played by her as the *decisive self*, without shadings, there was no monotony in her characterization. Interest for us was maintained throughout by changes of dynamics and tempo, by varying the intensity and rhythms of Medea's actions.

This was justified, because if ever a character was decisive to a degree where the other *selves* were submerged beyond hope of survival, it's Medea. The vulnerability that allowed her to feel grief at Jason's betrayal, or love for her children, by the end of the play is engulfed in the ocean of her hatred. Her instinct to strike out blindly could not stand up against her calculating, shrewd decision to hurt Jason and her other enemies where they lived. She played for time in which to develop her revenge, but she wore no mask as *social self*. She was Medea—a princess, a sorceress, almost a goddess—and she did what she did without excuse to Jason and the rest of the world. Few characters are so capable of suppressing their other *selves*, their emotional subtleties.

HENRY V

This is one of the greatest roles in all of Shakespeare's history plays. Picking up where *Henry IV, Part 2* left off, we now see Prince Hal as the new King Henry. Many consider Laurence Olivier's film portrayal to be definitive. Recently, Kenneth Branagh, a young British actor, has garnered acclaim in his own film version that, like Olivier, he directed himself. Not withstanding such precedents, Tom decided to try his hand at the role. This was his summary:

Henry has come to the throne of England with the resolve to be a mature sovereign and put behind him his wild youth. Insulted by the Dauphin's mockery of times he wants to forget, Henry is triggered to act on his belief that he has a right to various French domains. He inspires his armies to win the day in France against great odds. He secures his acquisitions for England and himself by marrying Katherine, the French king's daughter, with whom he conveniently falls in love.

Tom's list of clue words and phrases followed:

> Natural leader, man of action, demagogue, powerful, charismatic, courageous, risk taking, hot-headed, impulsive, proud, self-righteous, arrogant, egocentric, direct, intelligent, passionate, humorous, self-justifying.

I then asked Tom what *self* he thought dominated Henry's actions. He reasoned that Henry was predominately a *decisive self*, "The way he reacts to the insult—at that point the whole future is determined," Tom stated. "There are other *selves*, of course, but Henry won't let them affect his decision to go ahead with his plans."

Armed with his choice of subjects, Tom went off to Tune Up, try a *decisive self* exercise, and do his Exploration. He reported back having had the following experience:

> I started as fire burning, the movement of the flames. I felt the breathing of the oxygen, driving the flames higher. I became the breath—in . . . out . . . —fanning the flames. I was wind, blowing, gusting, in and about everything on the ground below me. I became a strong southeast wind. The wind rushed, ran. My forces went against the corners of these walls, around the pillars, driving, lashing out here, swirling there. I was running, running. A lion. Wind blew across grasses. A lion. Gusts bent the tall savannah grass. Light, springy, powerful. Leaping, dashing, quick. I could feel the sinews beneath my skin. As I ran, I could turn in an instant. Leaping, turning. Stop. Go. A motorcycle. Hot. Revving, waiting for the gas. Straining against the instant of acceleration. What a blast! I popped a wheelie. Accelerated straight toward a wall. Turn, swerve.
>
> After I had explored all three existences, I let them run together, one emerging after another. Sometimes together. Legs of lion, shoulders and head wind, hands breezes, feet wheels.

This was certainly an active Exploration, but you'll notice it was very much on one note. You should always let what happens happen and if you want to try enriching your physicalization, add more subjects, or alter the ones you selected.

Nancy's Medea and Tom's Henry were both clearly decisive characters in their scenes. After having watched Henry as Tom played him, I asked Nancy what differences she thought were most evident in the two decisive characters?

"Medea is Medea—that's the way she is. It never occurs to her to account for her actions or defend herself," Nancy explained. "I don't think Tom's Henry was like that at all."

Tom concurred. "Being a leader, Henry has to control his followers, to calculate, to manipulate them. He explains to them whatever he wants to explain, or whenever it is in his interest to explain." As for Medea, he didn't think "Medea cared anything about being a leader."

Nancy picked out a strong distinction between the two characters, "Henry could be impulsive and hot-headed at times; Medea had nothing impulsive about her at all. She was obsessed in her focus on Jason's destruction; Henry would consider the consequences of his decisions."

Both actors had a ball playing these full-tempered roles. Tom especially enjoyed Henry's sense of humor, which Nancy found in Medea to be that of an army tank's.

I then asked my students if they could think of other characters dominated by their *decisive self*. Amy immediately thought of Lady Macbeth. But she saw her as very different from Medea, who only "wanted revenge—Lady Macbeth wanted the throne for her husband and herself." Amy thought Lady Macbeth was more like Henry, in fact, especially, she said, "in her ambition for power. But I don't think Henry would murder his friends to reach his goal, and Lady Macbeth would murder anybody."

Bill's choice was Richard III. "He would also murder anyone to get the throne and keep it," Bill offered. "He made up his mind about what he wanted and he went for it in a straight line, loving every minute of it."

Carol mentioned both Antigone and Creon. "According to Sophocles, these were two of the most stubborn, decisive characters ever created," she told us. But Carol believed they were similar only in their decisiveness. "Creon made the law that no one was to bury Antigone's brother, Oedipus's son, who had risen against him. Antigone went right ahead and buried him anyway. For her, the laws of God decreeing proper burial superseded man-made law." She summed up their relationship with the dictum, "It was the irresistible force meeting the immovable object. Neither would give an inch."

The list could go on and on. Another student suggested Ben and Regina from Lillian Hellman's *The Little Foxes*. Frank, who played the valet to Susan's Miss Julie, thought Jean was a decisive character. The point is that a wide variety of very different people may be dominated by the same trait. It is just as important to note how your character is unique as it is to find the role's common aspect.

LOOKING BACK

"Creating a Character" has integrated your emotional identification and your physical transformation with a character as set forth by the author in the text of a play. Having gone step-by-step through these studies, you are aware there has been a definite progression toward that goal.

Through these twelve example roles, it should be clear how you find the *self* in the play as a whole or in a particular scene, and how you connect with that *self* on a visceral level. You understand how your feeling about this *self* influences your choice of subjects for Exploration, and how this Exploration then provides you with the nuances and shadings to make your characterization viable.

The more you concentrate on these techniques, the more you will absorb them. They will become a natural, integral part of the way you work on a character.

19

Looking Forward

The final stage of physicalizing a character brings you to the beginning of a lifetime of work, to perceiving the characteristics and patterns of all sorts of people. Become a lifelong observer of other people, your fellows, learning to understand with your feelings the truth of their nature.

Although you must observe to know the character's manners and actions and reactions in varying situations, the mechanisms of your observation cannot be forced. Because your aim is to identify with the character in its totality, you cannot direct your attention now to this detail, now to that. Observation is a state of semi-consciousness in which you absorb information unfocused, without intent.

A baby observes, but he is unaware of it. A baby, watching us without focusing, is lost in our actions, in whatever we are doing. His lips move unconsciously when we talk; his hands, when we gesture. When he begins an intentional action of his own, we know his moment of observation is over. Put yourself in a neutral state. Become this "emptiness" within which the life you observe takes shape. Observe like the baby.

Just as musicians and dancers practice to keep up their technique and muscle tone, you must practice daily. The process of learning is as endless as the scope of human character and activity.

Seek the complexity of emotions, expressions, and layers of meaning that rich, true characterizations can bring to an audience. Always look below the surface for the "truth" of the character.

Truth may have more than one face. There is no right or wrong in understanding a play. All interpretation, by definition, is subjective. A great play is open to differing interpretations and therefore always fresh.

There is no one definitive way to play Hamlet, for example. John Gielgud's portrayal, or Laurence Olivier's, or Richard Burton's, or Nicol Williamson's, or Derek Jacobi's, or Kevin Kline's—all have their supporters who claim that their favorite actor has revealed the ultimate truth. And for them, such is the case. But times change, personalities differ, and ambiguities may have more than one resolution. Joel Grey says the twenty years that elapsed since he was first acclaimed as the master of ceremonies in *Cabaret* helped him to grow into the role for its revival. Yul Brynner said that every performance as the king in *The King and I* brought him new insights. For both, their original, successful truth was not their ultimate truth.

The investment of yourself into the truth of a character does not necessarily mean losing your personal identity. Quite the contrary. Your personality emerges far richer than before. But you have also learned that no matter how strong your personality, the character is always the focus, the product of your art.

Actors, for some reason, seem reluctant to speak of theater as an art form and of themselves as artists. Yet it is as artists that we are dedicated to bringing the theater to life, and we express humanity's innermost drives through our art of acting.

I hope that this practical, workable book will be for you, the actor, a guide and inspiration.

Tuning Up Exercises

These exercises should be practiced before all sessions in Part II and Part III. They will ready you physically and clear your mind of distractions so that you can commit yourself fully to your Exploration. Tuning Up consists of three steps: centering, release, and ignition. Within each step you work on your breath, your voice, and your body. Before you begin, make sure you're familiar with the theoretical basis for each exercise. Each step is explained thoroughly in Chapter 8.

CENTERING

The purpose of these exercises is to gather and locate the centers of your physical resources, placing breath, voice, and body where each belongs. The aim of this process is the attainment of a certain neutrality.

Practice these centering exercises as explained, without varying the order in which you find them. Develop the breath, voice, and body separately, before moving on to work on all three in combination. Remember, these exercises have a natural flow, one into the other. In these exercises breath counts and position counts are indicated in odd numbers. As strange as it may sound, I have found that even numbers tend to dull the focus and diminish interest. Odd numbers seem to keep the senses alert and expectant.

Centering is practiced the same way for the three sections in Part II—*elements of nature, animals,* and *man-made objects*—as well as for the Combination Explorations you'll find in Part III.

Breath Centering

All exercises are supported and activated by correct breathing. For best results, you should know how to place your breathing in its centers. Breath centers are collection and distribution points for air. At each of these centers, air can be held or passed along.

When you inhale, the air always flows through the same channels to the lungs via the breath centers, whether or not these centers have been trained to expand their capacity.

How do you recognize your breath centers? They are the places in the body that react to certain sounds.

How will using these sounds locate your centers? They set up vibrations you can feel in the corresponding cavities of the body.

Visualize these breath centers, these cavities, to be like empty drums to be filled with air. Imagine the air you inhale being deposited in your abdominal cavity and then, like a flow of water, being pumped smoothly to higher levels, as if in a series of canal locks, until you feel the oxygen pumped to every part of your body.

Breathing in all the following exercises is through the nostrils and is calm and unhurried. Begin by sitting in a comfortable chair or on the floor. Lean against the back of the chair or the wall to keep your spine straight and muscular tensions to a minimum.

First Breath Center (abdomen).　Inhale into the abdomen until it can contain no more air. Hold the air there for five counts. Exhale slowly until the cavity is empty of air.

Second Breath Center (chest).　As before, inhale into the abdominal cavity, but continue until the chest is full of air also. Do not raise the shoulders. Raised shoulders constrict the throat and block the air flow. The chest is not full until the rib cage expands sideways as well as outward from the breastbone. Hold the air in both abdomen and chest for a total count of five. Then exhale slowly, starting with the abdomen, until both cavities are emptied of air.

Third Breath Center (lower throat).   Repeat as before, but bring the air as far as the lower throat. Release the air in the established pattern.

Fourth Breath Center (upper throat).   Repeat, continuing to the upper throat.

Fifth Breath Center (sinus cavity between the eyebrows).   Repeat, continuing to the sinuses.

Sixth Breath Center (top of the cranium).   Repeat, continuing to the top of the skull.

Flood.   In one deep, rapid inhalation, flood all six breath centers with air simultaneously. Hold the air for a five-count. Exhale slowly.

Voice Centering

Your vocal centers are the same as your breath centers—the abdomen, the chest, the lower throat, the upper throat, the sinus cavity between the eyebrows, and the top of the head. In order to use your voice with maximum ease, variety, and effectiveness, you must learn to control your voice from its centers. There are specific sounds to guide you to your vocal centers. Why have I selected these particular sounds? Over the years, as I have explored many systems which analyze sound, I have found that for the actor's purposes some of the yogic systems come closest to being of the most practical benefit. In this instance, I have discarded those elements which are not relevant to the actor and developed those which help find the vocal centers and utilize them to the maximum.

What are these sounds? They are:

- <u>Ah</u> as in father
- <u>Oo</u> as in too
- <u>O</u> as in so
- <u>Ee</u> as in we
- <u>N</u>
- <u>M</u>

The first four are pure vowel sounds in that each sound is distinct and separate from any other vowel sound. Diphthongs—combinations of vowels such as I which is made of Ah plus E, or OY which is O plus E—are not used here. They will disperse your vocal energies instead of focusing them. The two consonants, N and M will guide you to the other vocal centers.

While we are interested only in the pure sounds themselves, if you precede them with another sound, the voice will emanate smoothly without creating pressure on the vocal chords: hAh, yOO, sO, wE, suN, and suM.

Each of the six sounds should be practiced separately. Sit in a comfortable position, on a chair or the floor, leaning against a support to avoid strain. Be sure your spine is straight but not tense. The vocal chords, throat, and chest are free of muscular tension. There are three steps:

1. Gently place the fingertips of both hands on the appropriate center for the given sound.

- For hAh, the center is the abdomen.
- For yOO, the center is the middle of the chest.
- For sO, the center is the lower throat.
- For wE, the center is the upper throat. (Here, touch the throat with your thumbs and temples with your index fingers)
- For suN, the center is the lower part of the forehead between the eyebrows.
- For suM, the center is the top of the head.

2. Inhale deeply.

3. Make the given sound, extending it smoothly and evenly, until you are completely empty of breath.

- For hAh, open the mouth as if you are yawning, with the lower jaw relaxed and the tip of the tongue lightly touching the gum close to the lower teeth.
- For yOO, make a small opening between round, pursed lips. Otherwise the action is the same as above.
- For sO, the lips are round but the opening is larger. Otherwise the action is the same as above.

- For wE, pull the lips wide, as if in a grin. Once you have found the sound, continue it, relaxing the grin. Otherwise the action is the same.
- For suN, open the mouth wide with the lower jaw relaxed and the tip of the tongue lightly touching the upper palate near the teeth.
- For suM, relax the tongue and lower jaw, keeping the lips together.

After you've gone through this process with each of the six sounds, you're ready to move on to the following exercises.

Floating 1.   Remain in a comfortable sitting position and visualize the ocean. It is calm, blue, and undisturbed. As before, inhale deeply and produce the first basic sound, hAh, from its center. Place the sound on the water nearby. Send it gently floating away upon the blue until it reaches the horizon. Let the sound stay there until you have exhaled completely.

Floating 2.   Inhale deeply. This time place the sound all the way out on the horizon right from the beginning. Then bring the sound floating back, closer and closer, until it rests in its center.

Floating 3.   Send the sound out to the horizon as in Floating 1. Then bring the sound back to its center, as in Floating 2. Using the same procedure, work on each of the other five sounds.

Body Centering

Because every part of your body is where it belongs, each part is already centered. Therefore, in body centering the purpose of the exercises is to collect energy in its central source—the solar plexus. From this center the appropriate amount of energy is distributed as needed to every part of the body.

The Basic "A" Position.   The A position is the position you assume to attain neutrality. You lie on your back on the floor, arms and legs opened diagonally at a forty-five degree angle from your spine. Your body is in the approximate shape of the letter A (see figure 1). You should be relaxed, letting the floor bear your weight.

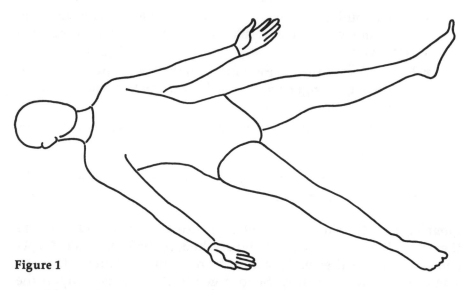

Figure 1

The palms are always open, facing upward. Some Eastern philosophies hold that the palms receive energy that then penetrates the body. When the palms rest on the floor, the energy of the body flows out through the hands and down into the ground. Without necessarily subscribing to these ideas, I have found that having the palms face up is more effective in energizing the body.

The Basic "i" Position.   The i position is the position you assume lying on your back on the floor with arms close to the sides and legs together. Your palms should comfortably against your thighs. This is the shape of the small letter i, with the head representing the dot (see figure 2).

Body centering is always combined with breathing exercises. Each exercise begins in either the A or i position. After each exercise in this series, assume the A position until your breath regains its normal rhythm. All inhaling in this series is through the nose only. You exhale, however, through the mouth.

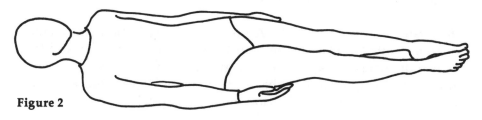

Figure 2

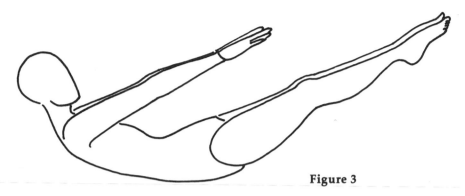

Figure 3

Fulcrum Stretched in "i."   In the i position, inhale for a count of three, raising the head, arms, chest, and legs eight inches above the floor, staring through the space between the big toes (see figure 3). Hold the breath in this position for a count of nine. Exhale and come back to the *i* position on the count of five.

Fulcrum Bent in "i."   In the i position, raise the head, arms, chest, and legs eight inches above the floor, this time with a gentle bend in the knees, elbows, and wrists, using as little muscle as possible, as you inhale for a count of three (see figure 4). Hold the position and breath for a count of seven and exhale, coming back to the i position on the count of five.

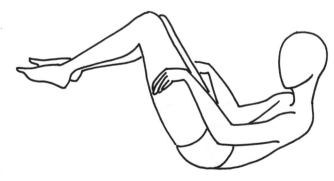

Figure 4

Figure 5

Fulcrum Stretched in "A." From the A position, bring the head, arms, chest, and legs eight inches above the floor as you inhale on a count of three. The legs and arms are extended forward (see figure 5). Hold the breath for nine counts. Then exhale for a count of five, returning to the A position.

Fulcrum Bent in "A." Stay in the A position, doing as you did in in the previous exercise, only now keep the knees, elbows, and wrists bent, as in the second exercise (see figure 6). Return to the A position as you exhale on a count of five.

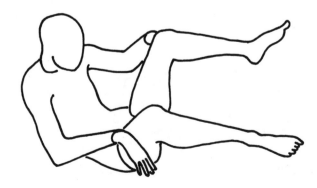

Figure 6

Fetus Floating. From the i position, curl up into a tight ball, while still lying on your back. Pull your thighs against your chest, and wrap your arms around your shins, and bend your head up against the knees. Inhale for a count of three. Hold for seven counts and exhale for a count of five, returning to the i position.

Fulcrum Prone in "i." Take the i position, face down. As you inhale for a count of three, raise yourself as high as you can off the floor, so your only contact with the ground is the area between your navel and pubic bone. Hold your breath and position for a seven-count, then exhale for a count of five, as you return to the i position.

Fulcrum Prone, Legs in "A," Arms in "V." Take the A position, face down, repeating the previous exercise's procedure, but here the arms are extended diagonally before you, as in a V (see figure 7). Hold for a seven-count, then exhale on the count of five, returning to the original prone position.

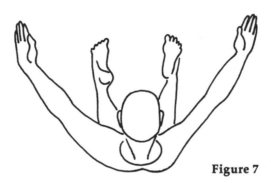

Figure 7

Fetus Sitting. From the i position, sit up, inhaling on the count of three, collecting the entire body tightly in a ball—thighs against the chest, arms wrapped around the shins, forehead on the knees, and feet on the floor under the buttocks. Hold the breath and position for seven counts. Repeat this exercise twice, for a total of three times.

RELEASE

The release exercises are designed to rid the actor of any residual tensions that are brought from the actor's life outside the theatre.

Remember, this is an active relaxation; the release shouldn't relax you so you become dulled or soporific. These exercises should fill you with positive, creative energy.

Breath Release

1. Sitting comfortably, inhale deeply through your nose, sending the air slowly to your breath centers. When they all are full, hold your breath, count to five, then exhale all at once through the nose.

2. Reverse the procedure described above, inhaling at once and exhaling slowly and gradually. This is also done through the nose.

3. Inhale slowly through the nose. Count to five, holding the breath. Exhale at once, this time through the open mouth.

4. Inhale at once through the nose. Count to five, holding the breath. Exhale slowly through the open mouth.

5. Repeat Exercises 3 and 4 twice in succession.

Voice Release

1. Yawn easily and freely, with the mouth open wide. It should feel good.

2. Inhale comfortably and deeply, then sigh. Be careful to release the sigh freely, without forcing it or catching it in the throat.

3. Inhale deeply. Whisper each basic sound (hAh, yOO, sO, wE, suN, suM) in the usual order. Be careful not to scratch the vocal chords. Learn to produce the whispers without straining.

4. With full voice, make a chain of the basic sounds in the same order, evenly, one after the other in the same breath. Keep repeating the chain until you have exhaled completely.

5. With full voice, make a chain of the basic sounds in order, one at a time. Start at the abdominal cavity with hAh and raise the pitch as each sound climbs to a higher cavity, ending with suM at the top of the head.

6. Repeat Exercise 4, but raise the pitch as in Exercise 5.

7. Tilt the head back slightly, opening the mouth wide. Imagine yourself to be a water container, brimful from the abdomen to the

lips. Spew out the "water" all at once. Don't inhibit any natural sound that comes out with the "water."

8. Again, imagine yourself as containing water. This time let it drain slowly from the mouth until you are empty. The sound that accompanies the voiding of the "water" should be free and natural.

Body Release

Prayer 1.　　Kneeling on the floor, rest your buttocks on your heels. Hold the torso loose, leaning somewhat forward. Remaining on the knees, straighten up as you rise from the heels, stretching the arms upward and inhaling for a count of seven (see figure 8). Hold the breath for a count of seven, then let the breath and voice go all at once as you fall back into your original position.

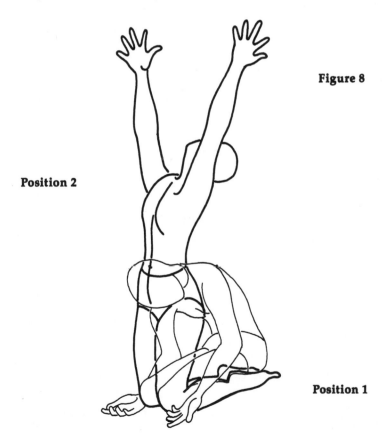

Figure 8

Position 2

Position 1

Prayer 2.   This exercise is similar to Prayer 1, except for the breathing. Now stretch, inhaling at once. Hold the breath for a count of seven and exhale for a seven-count as you fall back into a kneeling position with the forehead touching the floor.

Fulcrum, Granite.   In the A position on the floor, exhale until you are empty. As you inhale all at once, immediately tense the entire body rock-hard, with fists tight, arms and legs tight and off the floor, facial muscles tight, and so on. Every muscle should be contracted to its limit. Hold this position and the breath for seven counts, then release all tensions at once and fall back with a scream that leaves you empty.

Fetus, Explosion.   In the A position, exhale until you are empty. As you inhale all at once, contract into a tight Fetus Floating position, every muscle tight and tensed to its utmost. Hold this position and the breath for seven counts and then explode, releasing the voice and the body simultaneously, without regard to how you may fall. Empty yourself completely. This exercise imposes no design on you. You are free to tense up according to what gives the best results and to explode in which ever way best suits your body.

IGNITION

Ignition leads directly to Exploration, as I mentioned earlier. Always begin this section with the same basic breath ignition exercises. The voice and body ignition exercises that follow, however, are individually designed to apply to *elements of nature, animals,* and *man-made objects.*

Basic Breath Ignition

These breath exercises direct the flow of oxygen to specific parts of your body, inundating your entire physical structure with energy, increasing your alertness, vitality, and focus. Do not accelerate the pace and force of your breathing until you have warmed up.

As you inhale, it is easy for you to feel the breath penetrating the body cavities which are the physical receptacles of your air. Believe it or not, you can breathe vitality into every part of your structure, even into your toes. This concept—that the breath can be sent throughout the body—is an important one to grasp. As an actor, in order to make your toes as well as every other part function to maximum advantage, summon your imagination and power of concentration to breathe air into your toes, your feet, your legs, your torso, your fingers, your arms.

Breathe only through the nose. Begin by lying in the A position on the floor with your eyes closed. Inhale deeply once, then exhale completely. Remain calm until the breathing resumes its natural rhythms.

Inhale, sending the air directly to the toes and going up to the top of the head in one breath, through the feet, lower legs, knees, thighs, genitalia, buttocks, abdomen, chest, throat, fingers, hands, lower arms, elbows, armpits, shoulders, back of head, entire head. Exhale the same way, beginning with the toes. This should be done several times, all the while your body should lay relaxed on the floor. No motion is necessary. After you've oxygenated your entire body, move on to the next step in breath ignition.

Breath of Fire. In these exercises—the most energizing of all the breath exercises—sit comfortably with eyes closed. Inhale and exhale through the nose.

1. Inhale with sharp, fast, staccato breaths until you can't take in any more air. Exhale in slow motion.

2. Repeat the previous exercise, but inhale in slow motion and exhale in staccato breaths.

3. Inhale and exhale in staccato.

4. Breathe in and out fast and lightly, panting like a dog but through the nose only, never filling yourself completely with air. End with a fast, complete inhalation, count five, and then resume normal breathing for a few seconds.

5. Select one or more of the body centering positions and do these Breath of Fire exercises in each position.

Basic Voice Ignition

In voice centering, you used basic sounds to find your vocal centers. In voice release, you used your voice to relieve yourself of tensions. Now in voice ignition, you warm up your voice. You look for and discover the flexibility, volume, and shades of which the voice is capable, and train it to respond to the needs of the Exploration. To "ignite" through the voice, search for the sound best able to execute your own concept of your given subject of Exploration. Do the voice ignition exercise below for your subject category. Then skip right to the appropriate body ignition exercise before beginning your Exploration.

Elements of Nature.   Make a variety of specific nature sounds: wind, waves, thunder, an avalanche, a volcano, a hissing river, rain. Next, make specific sounds based on the particular subject of your Exploration. For example, if your subject is a cloud, make a sound with ample, wide-open mouth, concretizing the sound by letting it go freely from its source as if out into a vacuum. From right to left, the sound floats gently in the limbo of space. Or, if your subject is to be thunder, imagine thunder cracking overhead and produce sounds accordingly.

Animals.   Make the sounds of different animals: lions, horses, elephants, birds, bees. Then try to make specific sounds based on the particular subject of the Exploration.

Man-Made Objects.   Make the sounds of man-made objects: clocks, metronomes, cars, toasters, sirens, planes, cannons, machine guns, musical instruments. Then try making sounds inspired by the object you've chosen.

Body Ignition

Do the exercises appropriate to your subject category immediately after the corresponding voice ignition. All this body work is to be done with free breathing and any vocal sounds you feel like making.

Elements of Nature

In all the following exercises, except for the log rolls, begin with the Fulcrum in A position.

Hard Shake.   All at once, shake your entire body furiously.

Soft Shake.   The same as the Hard Shake, but the shaking is less violent.

Undulation.   As above, only now your movements are as if you are waving under water.

Prone Hard Shake.   From Fulcrum Prone in A, shake yourself hard, as in the first exercise, but face down.

Prone Soft Shake.   As above, but with less violent shaking.

Prone Undulation.   As above, but with the wave-like movement of the third exercise.

Log Roll Hard Stretch.   Stretch out on the floor on your back, arms above the head, touching the floor. With your muscles as hard as a tree trunk, roll to one side of the room and then to the other.

Log Roll Soft Stretch.   Repeat the action of the previous exercise, but with the muscles more relaxed.

Animals

Foot Bite I.   From the A position, immediately contract your body and grasp your right foot with both your hands, moving your head as close to the big toe as you can. If possible, nibble the toe gently.

Foot Bite II.   Repeat the above exercise, but with the left foot.

Foot Bite III.   Repeat, but now grasp both feet and try to nibble both toes simultaneously.

Foot Bite IV, Prone.   Repeat the first exercise, only now try it lying on your stomach. If you are not as flexible as a contortionist, you cannot achieve the actual foot bite, but go as far as you can with the idea of biting.

Foot Bite V, Prone.   Try nibbling the other foot while lying on your stomach.

Foot Bite VI, Prone.   Repeat as above, but with both feet.

Bow Fish I.   In the i position, curve to one side, trying to touch your toes with the top of your head. At all times, stay on your back, face to the ceiling. Arch as far as you can.

Bow Fish II.   Repeat the previous exercise, only curving to the other side.

Bow Fish III, Prone.   Once again, curve to one side trying to touch the top of your head to your toes, only this time try from the i position, face down.

Bow Fish IV, Prone.   The same as above, only curve to the other side.

Bow Fish V, Swim.   From the i position, curve smoothly in one continuous motion from one side to the other, as if you're a fish swimming through the water.

Bow Fish VI, Swim Prone.   Repeat the above exercise, but face down, on your stomach.

Long Bridge i.   From the i position, supported only by the top of your head, your elbows, and your feet on the floor, lift up your entire body (see figure 9).

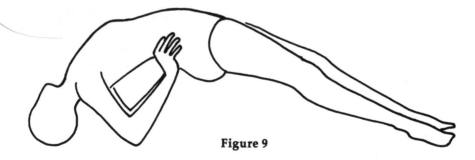

Figure 9

Long Bridge i, Prone.   Repeat the previous exercise, but face down, on your stomach (see figure 10).

Side Bridge i.   Lie on your right side. Pushing up with your right hand and arm, lift your body to curve upward off the floor until only your right hand and foot maintain contact with the floor.

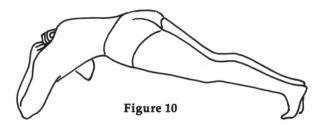

Figure 10

Side Bridge ii.   Lie on your left side and lift your body upward off the floor until you're supported by only your left hand and foot.

Man-Made Objects

Fetus Swaying.   As in Fetus Floating (see body centering exercise), start on your back, and bring your knees up to your chest and your forehead to your knees. Curled up in this position, sway on the floor from left to right, one side to the other, for about a minute.

Fetus Rolling.   Starting in the same curled position as above, roll from one side of the room to the other, and then back again.

Fetus Rocking.   From the Fetus Sitting position (see body centering exercise), rock backward and forward.

Fetus Somersaulting.   From the previous exercise's position, continue the rocking motion forward and roll from one end of the room to the other. Then roll backward.

FOR FURTHER STUDY

Because of time constraints, only a selection of the possible exercises can be done in each session. Below are some further voice and body ignition exercises.

The voice exercises fall into three categories: for individuals, for pairs, and for groups. All of the body exercises are designed for a group of actors. In each category, select only those applicable to your specific study for the session. These extra workouts should help prevent you from falling into repetitive patterns that dull your spontaneity.

Voice Ignition: Individuals

The Crazies.   Make a free series of "crazy" sounds—snoring, tongue-clicking, lip-blowing, bubbling, hooting, and so on.

Globe.   Create an ample hAh sound, and visualizing a huge globe, caress it with your sound, wrapping your arms around it.

Harpoon.   Make a sharp tight yOO sound. Use it like a harpoon, and imagine a direct hit on a nearby target.

Waltz.   Make an ample sO sound. Keep the sound moving as if you are following a waltzing couple around a dance floor.

Swing.   Make a sharp, direct wE sound. Shoot it out as if to hit a moving swing. Imagine that the sound sticks and flies to and fro, from left to right. Try not to ever let the sound you're making fall below your mouth level.

Self-Dialogue.   Produce sounds from two different centers as if they're having a dialogue. Use all the basic sounds in their several centers in a variety of combinations. Then merge all the sounds.

Target Shooting I.   Choose targets at two different distances in the room. Shoot your sound directly to one and then to the other in one breath, alternating targets until you have exhaled completely. Try this once each with the sounds hAh, yOO, sO, and wE.

Target Shooting II.   Repeat the previous exercise but choose only one target. This time, don't wait until you've completely exhaled, but kill the sound at the second of impact.

Corner.   Shoot each of the four sounds from the previous exercise to a corner of the room and let the sound stay there until you've finished the breath.

Wall Bounce.   Standing close to the wall, shoot the sound at it, making it bounce off the wall to the opposite side of the room.

Floor Bounce.   Shoot each sound onto the floor and make it bounce off the ceiling.

Voice Ignition: Partners

Dialogue.   You and your partner stand at opposite ends of the room from each other. Create a dialogue from various sound centers. If you begin with hAh, your partner might respond with wE, and so forth.

Touch.   Touch your partner with various parts of your body, then detach yourself and make the sound of the touch sensation.

Sphere.   Make the hAh sound, sending it to the middle of the room, creating a sphere. Your partner enters your sphere of sound, sensing the vibration and its limits. He or she should try leaving the sphere and reentering it.

Spheres.   Create four different spheres with the four basic vowel sounds. Your partner goes into one sphere, out of it into another and so on.

Dome.   Shoot a sound into the middle of the room, creating a dome there. Your partner, who is under the dome, shoots his own sound into it overhead, as if his own sound is a net like a spider's web. Your partner collects your sound in this web and brings it toward him/her, sucking it in and letting it come to rest deep within.

Voice Ignition: Group

Scale.   You are one of a group in which one person is designated as the working individual. The rest of you are dispersed at various distances from that person and are passive, receptive. The individual sends a sound toward you, then to another and another, in no prescribed order. The sound tends to shift on the scale as the distances to each targets vary. One need not be a singer to achieve this effect.

Square.   The group breaks up into foursomes. Each quartet creates a square with a member in each corner. All members produce any of the four vowel sounds simultaneously, each sending a sound to the other three members of the square.

Group Sphere.   An individual stands at the center of the room. The rest of you stand shoulder to shoulder in a tight line at one end of the room. Everyone in the line makes the same basic sound, creating a field of sound like a sphere around the individual. The individual, sensing the vibrations, leaves the sphere and reenters it.

Group Dome.   As in the previous exercise, the individual and the rest of you interact, but now, instead of a sphere, the sound creates a dome. The individual makes sucking noises to pull the dome into himself.

Unison.   Form a semi-circle around an individual group member who produces any sound he or she chooses. Repeat the sound, trying to adopt it.

Harmony.   Form a circle, with an individual in the center who produces a sound. Each group member answers in harmony as he or she sees fit. The response is not in unison but in harmony.

Basic Body Ignition (combined with voice): Group

This entire series of exercises is called *Leaders and Followers.* As members of the group, form two lines facing each other about twelve feet apart. You need enough space between the actors in the lines for free movement. Each line has its Leader, who is stationed at the end of one line, at its left, so that there is one Leader at each end.

Whatever Leader A does, A's followers repeat. B's followers echo Leader B. As we proceed with the work, the Leaders change. Leader A goes to the end of Line A and Leader B to the end of Line B. The first follower in Line B becomes the new Leader B. Eventually, every follower has a turn to be a Leader.

Act, or react, spontaneously and instinctively. Try not to tell a story or be literal. Even when you mirror the Leaders, mirror the spirit of what they do, not the exact form and sound they make. Remain as close in action to the leaders as you can, but don't give yourself the time to study their actions in detail. Repeat the action as if you had invented it. What you absorb, produce instantly, facing the opposite line.

Leader A always starts. His followers immediately pick up on his action, facing Line B. Leader B then performs, and his line immediately follows suit, confronting Line A.

Sound Alone I. Physical movement is not involved in this exercise. Leader A makes a sound. The A line follows. Then Leader B makes a sound that has no relationship to that of Leader A. Line B follows.

Sound Alone II: Harmonious Dialogue. Leader A makes a sound. Line A follows. Leader B makes a sound inspired by Leader A's sound and having a relationship to it in agreement and harmony. Line B follows.

Sound Alone III: Clashing Dialogue. Leader A makes a sound. Line A follows. Leader B makes a sound inspired by that of Leader A but clashing with it and contrasting. Line B follows.

Body Alone I, II, and III. Sound is not involved in these three exercises. Repeat the sound exercises, only the Leaders make physical gestures or movements instead of sound. The first time each Leader makes unrelated movements. The second time the movement should be inspired by the other Leader. The third time the gesture should contrast or clash with that of the other Leader.

Sound and Body Together I, II, and III. Now do the same three exercises, only each Leader combines a sound and a physical movement into one gesture which each line's followers repeat.

Appendix 2

Further Reading

Acting Is Believing: A Basic Method, Charles McGaw and Larry D. Clark, Holt, Rinehart and Winston, 1987.

> Primarily a textbook which culls its exercises from everyone from Stanislavsky to Marowitz.

The Act of Being: Towards a Theory of Acting, Charles Marowitz, Taplinger Publishing Company, 1978.

> Written by the former artistic director of the Open Space Theatre, one of London's leading experimental theatres in the late 1960s and '70s. Included are all sorts of exercises for every part of the acting process—a stretch for actors on all levels.

Advice to the Players, Robert Lewis, Theatre Communications Group, 1989.

> This is an eclectic approach to acting written by a one-time Group Theatre member and former head of Yale School of Drama's acting program. Many detailed exercises are included that will sharpen relaxation, imagination, and improvisation techniques.

Building a Character and **My Life in Art**, Constantin Stanislavsky, Routledge, Chapman & Hall, 1989.

Read these books again to better understand this revolutionary acting technique—classic, yet most modern. <u>Must</u> books for every serious actor.

A Dream of Passion: The Development of the Method, Lee Strasberg, New American Library, 1988.

Disregarding the defensive approach, the book brilliantly clarifies what seemed vague and evasive about the Strasberg "method." Invaluable insights are scattered throughout.

Great Directors at Work: Stanislavsky, Brecht, Kazan, Brook, David Richard Jones, University of California Press, 1986.

This is a deeply thoughtful analysis of these men's work. Rich in intelligent observations, the book is important not only for directors, but for actors as well, in order to understand how to develop a character within a specific style.

Impro: Improvisation & the Theatre, Keith Johnstone, Theatre Arts Books, 1979.

A book about the process of freeing the imagination and the physical instrument through the use of improvisational exercises.

Improvisation, John Hodgson and Ernest Richards, Grove Weidenfeld, 1987.

Includes techniques on how to develop observation, working with and without a text, and building a play through improvisation.

Improvisation for the Theatre: A Handbook of Teaching and Directing Techniques, Viola Spolin, Northwestern University Press, 1983.

Improvisation is the operative word in the title. The book is rich, specific, useful, and fun. Excellent for teachers.

No Acting Please!, Eric Morris and Joan Hotchkiss, Putnam Publishing Group, 1979.

This includes many group-oriented exercises geared to make the actor explore his or her feelings. You could call them the West Coast version of those most often used in the Method.

On Directing, Harold Clurman, Macmillan, 1974.

Though not designed specifically for the actor, this book is rich and informative with a world of insights from which the actor can benefit.

On Method Acting, Edward D. Easty, Ivy Books, 1989.

Some physicalization and animal exercises are included here, but mostly in the form of descriptive anecdotes about Method acting.

Playing: An Introduction to Acting, Paul Kuritz, University Press of America, 1989.

The purpose of this book is to reintroduce the actor to the forms of play used by children.

A Practical Handbook for the Actor, Melissa Bruder, Random House, 1986.

This is a very general book for beginners who want a text they can go through quickly.

The Rediscovery of Style, Michel Saint-Denis, Theatre Arts Books, 1960.

A short, incisive, important book about style in the theater.

Respect for Acting, Uta Hagen with Haskel Frankel, Macmillan, 1973.

A fine book filled with descriptions of sense memory and emotional memory exercises, concentrating on the physical details of characterization.

Sanford Meisner on Acting, Sanford Meisner and Dennis Longwell, Random House, 1987.

Though deceptive in its simplicity, this book is thorough in its focus on your finding the actor within you through your concentration on your partner.

Strasberg's Method As Taught by Lorrie Hull, S. Lorraine Hull, Ox Bow Publishing, 1985.

A combination of history and interpretation of the Method as taught by Ms. Hull, the exercises focus on relaxation, sense memory, affective memory, object, gibberish, song and dance, and improvisational techniques.

The Technique of Acting, Stella Adler, Bantam Books, 1988.

A straightforward, step-by-step, concise, practical, and comprehensive acting technique, with a deep understanding of human behavior.

To the Actor: On the Technique of Acting, Michael Chekhov, Harper & Row, 1985.

> Excellent essays on acting as an art form and on the actor as artist.

Towards a Poor Theatre, Jerzy Grotowski, Simon and Schuster, 1970.

> Physical exercises are included in the Polish director's book that are designed to align and harmonize the actor's body. Animal and plant images are used very specifically.

Training an Actor: The Stanislavski System in Class, Sonia Moore, Penguin Books, 1979.

> Based on taped recordings of Sonia Moore's classes, this book explores Stanislavsky's internal and external techniques as the students work through their scenes with his classic exercises.

The Transpersonal Actor: The Whole Person in Acting, Ned Manderino, Manderino Books, 1977.

> Sensory, animal, object, and inner monologue exercises are included in this "New Age" approach to acting.

Zen in the Art of Archery, Eugen Herrigel, Random House, 1989.

> This book was the greatest influence in my developing the technique of identifying with a character. Its exploration of methods to rid yourself of ego as you become one with the perfection of the instrument can be applied to acting.

Session Structures

LOOKING IN

The structure of each self session is described below.

Vulnerable Self (Minimum number of sessions suggested—8)

1) Sharing the Experience (40 minutes)
2) Tuning In: Forces of Nature (20 minutes)
3) Focus on Personal Vulnerability (30 minutes)
   a) Magnifying the Flaw
   b) Physicalizing the Flaw
4) Practice (between session work)

Instinctive Self (Minimum number of sessions suggested—4)

1) Tuning In: Exercising the Instinct (15–20 minutes)
   Run-freeze exercises; group zig zag exercises.
2) Triggering: Stimulating Instinctive reactions (45 minutes)
   Touch, Hearing, Sight, or Smell

Social Self (Minimum number of sessions suggested—3)

1) Tuning In: Exploring Emotions Unmasked (30 minutes for three pairs)

2) Exploring the Masking of Emotions (30 minutes for three sets of situations)
   a) Situations related to preceding Tuning In work
   b) Situations unrelated to preceding Tuning In work

Trusting Self (Minimum number of sessions suggested—3)

1) Tuning In: Surrendering the Body (15–20 minutes)
   The Trampoline; The Balloon; The Magnet
2) Situations (30–40 minutes)
   The Rowboat; The Shower; The Inner Song

Unresolved Self (Minimum number of sessions suggested—3)

1) Tuning In: Physical Indecision (15–20 minutes)
   Pulling; Non-Contact Pulling; The Snail's Antennae
2) Situations (45 minutes)
   The Tightrope; The Weightlifter; The Carpenter; The Pianist; The Actor; The Hunter

Decisive Self (Minimum number of sessions suggested—3)

1) Tuning In: Developing Self-Assertion and Focus (20 minutes)
   Assertion; Focus ("Follow-the-Left")
2) Situations from the Unresolved Self (30 minutes)
3) Situations not from the Unresolved Self (30 minutes)
   Walking; The Phone Call; The Confession; The Rebel; Firing a Friend

LOOKING OUT

All sessions follow the same basic five-step structure except where indicated under each heading.

Tuning Up (20–30 minutes)

1) Centering—Breath, Voice, and Body
2) Release—Breath, Voice, and Body
3) Ignition—Breath, Voice, and Body

Exploration (20–30 minutes)

1) Elements of Nature (minimum 6 sessions)
   Cloud; Fire; Darkness; Thunder; Ocean; Volcano

2) Animals (minimum 5 sessions)
   Water creatures; Reptiles; Insects; Birds; Mammals
3) Man-made Objects (minimum 3 sessions)
   Actor's choice

Contribution (25 minutes)

1) Preparation (10 minutes)
2) Presentation (15 minutes)

Discussion/Deduction (20 minutes)

1) Elements of Nature
   a) Discussion
   b) Group Clue Phrases
   c) Group Clue Words
   d) Individual Clue Words Written Down
   e) Three-sentence breakdown
2) Animals and Man-made Objects
   a) Discussion/Written reports
   b) Individual clue words and phrases underlined

Physicalization of a Character (20 minutes)

1) Preparation of situations
2) Presentation of ideal situation
3) Presentation of situation in conflict

CREATING A CHARACTER

There are two types of sessions in Part III: the primary session in which exploratory work is done; and the secondary session in which the actor works on a specific scene or monologue.

Preparation for Primary Class

1) Choose a role and read the play
2) Write a character summary
3) Write a list of clue words

Primary Class Session

1) Presenting the Preparation (10–20 minutes)
   a) Read summary and list of clue words

    b) Identify character's dominant *self*
    c) Choose three subjects for Exploration
  2) Tuning Up (30–35 minutes)
    a) Tuning Up exercises from Part II (20–25 minutes)
    b) Exercise from appropriate *self* chapter in Part I (10 minutes)
  3) Combination Exploration (25–35 minutes)

Secondary Class Session—Scene Work

Each actor should work on a number of different roles. Those included in this book are:

Blanche DuBois from *A Streetcar Named Desire*
Willy Loman from *Death of a Salesman*
Roberta from *Danny and the Deep Blue Sea*
Lee from *True West*
Arsinoë from *The Misanthrope*
Iago from *Othello*
Nora Helmer from *A Doll's House*
Lenny from *Of Mice and Men*
Julie from *Miss Julie*
Lopakhin from *The Cherry Orchard*
Medea from *Medea*
Henry from *Henry V*

NOTE: Times for all sessions in each phase of Part I, II, and III are approximate. Use your judgment according to your available time.

About the Authors

Moni Yakim began performing at age fourteen with the Massach Theatre in his native Jerusalem. In Paris, he studied with George Wilson at the Theatre Nationale Populaire, and with Tanya Bolashova. He studied mime with Marcel Marceau, and Etienne Decroux, in whose company he was a principal performer. In 1960, Mr. Yakim moved to the U.S. and founded the New York Pantomime Theatre with his wife Mina. They also created the Performance Theatre Center, for which he conceived, directed, and acted in many productions. Mr. Yakim directed the original production of *Jacques Brel Is Alive and Well* . . . Off-Broadway as well as on Broadway and abroad. He has directed at Yale Rep. and the American Shakespeare Festival (associate director), and has staged opera for the American Opera Center and the Metropolitan Opera Studio, among others. He created the movement for the movie *Robocop*, and its sequel, *Robocop II*.

As a teacher, Mr. Yakim has taught at the Stella Adler Conservatory, New York University, and Yale University, and has conducted master classes in Paris, Oslo, and Moscow. He currently teaches at the Circle in the Square Theatre School, The Juilliard Opera Center, and heads the movement department of the Juilliard Drama Division, where Mr. Yakim has taught since its founding in 1967.

Muriel Broadman has been a colleague and friend of Moni Yakim's for over twenty-five years, during which time she has written a half-dozen plays for his Performance Theatre Center. Her book, *Understanding Your Child's Entertainment* (Harper & Row) received a special citation from the Children's Theatre Association of America. She co-authored *Marionettes Onstage!*, which recently was reissued by Dover Press. She frequently contributes articles and reviews to *Back Stage*, as well as to other magazines, newspapers, and professional journals.